THE RESET SWITCH

THE RESET SWITCH

PINA DI DONATO

Copyright © 2020 Pina Di Donato

First published by the kind press, 2020

All rights reserved. No part of this book may be reproduced, stored in a retrieval system or transmitted in any form or by any means, electronic, mechanical photocopying, recording or otherwise, without written permission from the author and publisher.

This publication contains the opinions and ideas of its author. It is intended to provide helpful and informative material on the subjects addressed in the publication. While the publisher and author have used their best efforts in preparing this book, the material in this book is of the nature of general comment only. It is sold with the understanding that the author and publisher are not engaged in rendering medical, psychological advice or any other kind of personal professional service in the book. In the event that you use any of the information in this book for yourself, the author and the publisher assume no responsibility for your actions.

Cover and internal design by Nada Backovic
Illustrations by iStockphoto an Shutterstock
Photography credit HiSylvia Photography

 Cataloguing-in-Publication entry is available from the National Library Australia.

ISBN:978-0-6488706-3-0
ISBN: 978-0-6488706-4-7 (ebook)

To all those who illuminate my path and redirect me to the light when I venture off course, thank you for reminding me that brighter days are coming.

To all of the heroes of covid-19, thank you for your service.

Darkness cannot drive out darkness; only light can do that. Hate cannot drive out hate, only love can do that.

—MARTIN LUTHER KING JR, *Strength to Love*

CONTENTS

Preface xi
Acknowledgements xv
Introduction xix
A glitch in the system 1
An open letter to the universe 9
Why? 15
The remaining cobwebs 21
Many shades of light 31
When time stood still 41
The 'D' word 51
Ironically speaking 61
Twilight zone—season 2 71
An unexpected detour 83
Almost fifty and feeling fabulous 91
A word with my daughters 101
The path of least resistance 113
Connection matters 123
(Mother) Nature is calling 139
Trust your gut 151
Real versus manufactured 161
Follow the leader 171
From inside my cocoon 179
A glimmer of light 185
Epilogue 193
Endnotes 200
About the author 203

PREFACE

When I consider how far I have come in such a short time, I have to give myself a great big pinch. Yes, it's true that I have always wanted to publish a book. Not for the money (I don't think anyone actually does it for that), but for the sense of achievement and fulfilment that comes from seeing my words and my name in print. The fact that I am now the published author of two books completely blows me away. I have a very good imagination, but I must say that even mine didn't stretch quite this far. Well, not so soon anyway.

How did *The Reset Switch* come about? I have often asked myself that same question. Here I was, preparing for the launch of *Who Switched the Lights On?*, when all of the sudden I had a very strong feeling that I needed to write the next instalment. You see, much like you, this is not quite the year I thought I would be having. So many things had changed for me that by the end of 2019 I was quite excited about finally kissing that decade goodbye and preparing to give the next one a great big giant hug.

But then something happened. Something stepped in to spoil the party. Not just for me, but for all of us. The curtains had come down on our parade, quite unexpectedly, and our whole lives were put on pause.

And during the intermission, so many other things have caught our attention and stolen the limelight. The spotlight has been diverted to shine on a whole new and different-looking picture. Suddenly, we are seeing things we hadn't seen before. How can we go back to where we were, without rethinking the whole thing and making some important adjustments?

The world has been infected by a virus that none of us know very much about. It has infiltrated our lives, causing a major shutdown and a need to reset our systems. We have all been impacted in some way; some may not recover any time soon. Like many others out there, I suddenly found myself without a job. I had to work quickly to readjust my focus and reinvent myself. At times like these, you have to dig a little deeper than usual and get more creative. Never have I seen so many new ideas, inventions and new ways of just trying to get by in this challenging world. One thing we have all been given is a lot of time to make things happen. It's important to see this time as a gift and use it wisely. (And sure, like everyone else, I too have watched a hell of a lot of Netflix!)

We are currently being pushed to the limits of our thinking and our imaginations. The world is being tested like never before. This is a time that will go down in history as a major turning point, a major reset of humanity, and hence why I felt compelled to write about it.

Now that I am a writer, I have learnt to respect the creative process. It's important to capitalise on the times when ideas and information are flowing. Not every day is a good day to write. You don't get to pick and choose. But for some reason, while my first book was written over a lengthy period of time, this one turned out to be quite a quick download and a super quick turnaround.

Where to from here? Nobody really knows. Time will ultimately reveal the extent of the damage and how well we have done in passing this particular test. Much has come to light and many inconsistencies have been exposed. It appears there could be more here than meets the eye. There is no doubt that these aspects will continue to reveal themselves over time.

On the other hand, perhaps this is what we all needed. Could it be a blessing in disguise? By the way, great disguise, Universe, you certainly had me fooled!

I don't know about you, but I have unplugged everything. I am doing a full evaluation of what I have and what I need, and I am only going to reset the things that are truly necessary and which have the potential to add value to my life and the lives of those who occupy the special places around me.

To the special person reading this book: I hope you are doing okay. Thank you for coming along with me on this unique journey. I hope my views and perspective will provide you with a little comfort and shed some much-needed light on all that was, in the unprecedented year of 2020.

ACKNOWLEDGEMENTS

All of this can only happen when you have a publisher who has faith and belief in your abilities. A huge thank you, once again, to my editor and publisher, Natasha Gilmour, and all of the team at the kind press, who have the ability to make the whole process so natural, professional and seamless. Thank you also to Nada Backovic for designing such a superb book cover. I am so proud to have my name on such a great-looking book. You have an amazing talent.

It takes a village to write a book, even though it very much appears like a solo journey. It takes a whole support network comprised of professionals, family, friends, colleagues and peers. It also takes a community of followers and supporters who are willing to invest in your vision and buy your books.

A big thank you to my family and close friends who encourage me to pursue my love of writing. Thank you for all of the love and support you continue to show me. Thank you to those who lend me their ears to bounce off ideas and debate certain topics. And those who listened to me talk about whatever else I wanted to write. I very much appreciate your patience and enthusiasm.

Much less enthusiastic, but still quite proud, have been my three children, Luca, Alessia and Katia, who have been 'locked down' with me for the greater part of 2020. This has challenged all of us and on some days has driven us to the brink of despair. There have been many frustrations, some 'not too kind' words, and a few tears, but we seem to be making the most of this time. As the kids spend their time on 'remote learning', I spend my time immersed in all things books. I am so proud of the resilience they have shown and how they have approached the circumstances, particularly their learning. I am in awe of them!

I am also in awe of all of the people who have led us, protected us and cared for us during this crisis, in particular the frontline medical staff. As I say in the following pages, everyone is a hero in this particular story, and it would be amiss of me to not make special mention of all of the heroes, and pay tribute to all of the people worldwide who have lost their lives as a result of this nasty virus. My heart goes out to their loved ones. May we never forget them.

INTRODUCTION

I got out of bed this morning—well, it was actually closer to lunch time—feeling compelled to start writing a new book. This book. And one thing I have learnt is to take notice of messages that are loud and clear. This one was one of those!

And just in case I didn't get the message the first time, I was even hit with the title. How could I argue with that?

The reason I was still in bed at almost noon, which is so not like me, is that we are living in the most bizarre of times. We have been in self-isolation for much of the year. When I say *we*, I mean the collective *we*, as in the whole world. That is a whole new chapter, all on its own, likes scenes reminiscent of the movie *Twilight Zone*.

That's exactly where I have been lately: in the twilight. Neither here nor there, and often struggling to remember who I am and what my purpose is. 'There is no better use of this time than to write'… I hear that message coming to me from somewhere far, far away.

There are days when I feel it is difficult to string a sentence together, let alone something meaningful. Some days the creativity flows easily, and other days, I am so pensive and caught up in overthinking that the last thing I want to do is put pen to paper, or fingers to keyboard. But these highs and lows are precisely the perfect times to write. A true writer is brave enough to write from the light and the dark, and vulnerable enough to share it with the world.

Today, I am that person. Brave and vulnerable.

If you have read my first book, *Who Switched the Lights On?*, you will have already travelled with me through my process of awakening. I shared some of the insights that helped me through those times, and how I reconciled what was happening in a way that made sense to me and allowed me to grow through it.

It's ironic that I now find myself at yet another turning point in my life. With the closing of the chapters of my last phase, I entered a new one, which has brought about a whole new level of learning. I hope to learn the lessons a little faster this time, which should be the case, as I now consider myself a seasoned traveller.

Why am I writing another book so soon after the publication of my first? The answer is that I feel I have to. Just like an architect who designs a home. While that home is being built, she is busy designing the next one. That's what I have been doing.

With the current veil of darkness over the world, this point in time stands out to me as being an extremely significant time in history. In time, people will look back at these days in order to study what happened, how we dealt with it, and how this time enabled humanity to evolve. Will there ever be another time like this one? Possibly, but this fact does not diminish the importance of living in the present, and therefore documenting and learning from the events taking place on our collective doorsteps, right this minute.

Despite everything happening in the world right now, and what has happened to me personally, one of the things I have been blessed with is time. Time to focus on fulfilling some of the visions I have always seen in my dreams. So, right now, as time slows down just a little so I can catch my breath, I am making a conscious decision to play catch-up.

I am so pleased you are coming along with me as I set off on this new path. I hope we can leave some footprints and some cookie crumbs along the way. I can't promise what the ride will be like, at this stage, but if I have learnt anything from the past, it will be whatever we choose to make it.

From now on, we are going to take the path less travelled and the one of least resistance. This particular path is well lit in places and in others it is quite dark. We may stumble from time to time. We may find that we have inadvertently veered onto some gravel or become stuck in some mud. Some trees may fall and block our way, but we will find a way around those too. We may have to confront some shadows along the way. These will inevitably come to highlight some residual from the past that has not yet been dealt with. All of these challenges may slow down the process. It may take some extra effort to put ourselves back on track. But we will get back on it. Of this, I am completely and confidently certain.

Grab your backpack, decide what you're going to bring with you, and let's get moving ... oh, and don't forget your shiny crown. Where you are going, you are going to need it as a constant reminder of your value and your place in this world.

We should get going. Intermission will be over soon. We need to make sure we are prepared for the second act.

A GLITCH IN THE SYSTEM

Just because the lights have come on, on so many levels, it doesn't mean they don't flicker from time to time, decrease in intensity, or become dim. Sometimes, there may even be a temporary blackout. When things go dark, we need to search a little harder to find the light.

There does indeed appear to be a glitch in the system somewhere. A fault, a malfunction, a power surge. But it is not an isolated incident. It's not just at my place or your place; it seems to be everywhere.

The world has been plunged into darkness, and although we know it is temporary, it feels like it is lingering for a very long time. And who knows what will happen when the lights eventually come back on again. How will it all look? Will the lights be as bright as they were before? It will inevitably take some time before they can be restored to their former luminescence. Perhaps we won't want to go back to how we were. We may need to make some adjustments.

Many of us currently find ourselves stumbling around in the dark, hands patting down the walls trying so hard to find that damn switch that seems to be eluding us. The switch that has the potential to make all of our issues fade away. If only we could hit that reset switch.

And that is exactly what this is, in my opinion. If 2019 was indeed a time to reflect, re-evaluate and tidy up, then 2020 is definitely the time to reset. And whether we like it or not, we are being forced to do exactly that.

Resetting usually comes after a time when things have become unstuck. Something occurs which interrupts the usual flow or sequence. Just like my printer, which sometimes refuses to co-operate when things get backlogged and it just can't cope anymore. The quick fix is to cancel all of the print jobs, remove anything that may have become jammed in the machine, ensure it is all safe and clean, make any adjustments, and start again from the beginning, hoping that it will all work better the next time around. At times it may be enough to reset it from the power button. When I turn it back on, it goes through an initialisation sequence, a recalibration. It forgets everything it was doing prior to the reset. It fails to remember how it got so confused and overwhelmed by everything and it prepares to start again from scratch.

Sometimes, it's still not enough and we have to resort to something more drastic, which usually involves removing the plug from the wall altogether for a hard reset. And in the most extreme of circumstances, it may be time to just throw it in the bin and get a new one!

But the opportunity to reset gives us an opportunity to start again, and while that is the case, there is always hope.

More to the point, the bizarre circumstances of 2020 can more accurately be described like needing to reset a personal computer. We all know what impact a foreign virus can have on our PC if it gets infected. And unless you take steps to protect yourself from such an attack, it can create all sorts of problems. Just like our printers, our PCs also have a tendency to become overwhelmed and clogged and unable to meet all of the expectations imposed on them. Resetting is always the first thing you do to try to restore things to the way they used to be. The same goes with our phones and most technological devices.

This universal reset is a more difficult one, though. None of us were prepared for this invasion into our lives. We were oblivious. We thought we were invincible. But the events of today tell a very different story. We are in fact powerless in the face of an attack which we cannot foresee and where we cannot identify our opponent. We were not ready. We didn't have our defences up. We didn't have a contingency plan. We only had a management plan, and even that, against something as unpredictable as what we are facing, is struggling to fulfil its intended purpose.

It doesn't take much for order to completely go out the window, and systems to crumble under the mounting pressure. Even the experts are bewildered by this unwelcome visitor which has managed to make its way into every corner of the globe. Nobody is immune, there is no discrimination; everyone is susceptible.

And what results is a period of darkness, a time to cocoon ourselves once again. A time to think things through. To determine what's really important and to become more creative as we go back to basics for a little while.

Slow down, unplug, have a rest, prepare to reset. This is what we are being asked to do.

And, it is these in-between moments that can have significant impacts on one's life, some negative and some positive. In some cases, and increasingly so, there is no doubt that this is the worst thing that could have happened. Loss of employment, increase in anxiety, loss of meaningful connections to a workplace, family and friends. The increased reliance on alcohol and drugs as a means of coping. The effects on mental health and the consequences of increases in domestic violence are going to leave permanent scars on these generations. And that is the sad truth and the real facts of this matter.

We cannot change what is happening. All we can do is stay grounded and positive, and in continuous search of the light. We may need to lend a helping hand to those who are struggling to find that light. We will need to share some of ours or hold a torch for those who can't. We have to be kinder and more compassionate, and we have to genuinely care for one another, now more than ever before. We have to dig a little deeper. When the time finally comes to emerge from hibernation, the earth would have also benefited from the slow down and opportunity to rest. We will have restored and replenished some of what we had lost when we were too busy rushing around meeting all of the expectations imposed on us.

We are learning to make sacrifices and to go without. We are learning much more about ourselves and our power to overcome adversity. We are realising that our health, both mental and physical, is our greatest asset, and we have to try our best to preserve it at all costs. We are being asked to put our health and wellbeing above all else, even above our financial health. Such is its importance.

These are trying times, and we will all inevitably have some battle scars to show in the aftermath of these challenges.

So yes, it appears that we are dealing with a masked enemy, and it has cast a shadow over a year that by all accounts looked promising as it signalled the start of a new decade. But what this crisis has also uncovered is the deep divisions that exist within our society. It has uncovered the systems and the structures that no longer hold the same relevance. It has separated the weak from the strong, the quiet ones from the loud ones, the leaders from the followers. It has created greater contrasts between dark and light. It has illuminated many different aspects that needed to be made clear, and now we all have a responsibility to start cleaning up the mess.

Our search for the reset switch will ultimately be successful. The question is, are we prepared to make the long-lasting changes that need to be made? Or will we revert to our old ways? Will we learn the lessons, or will we be forced to repeat them until we do?

Isn't it amazing how different life looks now compared to what it looked like at the beginning of 2020? Let's go back to that time, just for a minute.

AN OPEN LETTER TO THE UNIVERSE

1 January 2020

Dear Universe

I write to you on the first day of a new year and a new decade. When I glance back over my shoulder at 2019, all I can say is, 'What was that?'

In what seemed like a whirlwind, I am surprised that I managed to pack in so many experiences, challenges and life-defining moments. It seems that the purpose of last year was a time to reflect, re-evaluate, tidy up and prepare to move forward. I get it!

I must say, Universe, you certainly do have a wicked sense of humour. The only problem is that I haven't always found it funny. On the contrary, you have often left me bewildered by your choices, and angered with the way you show me things and then tell me that I can't have them.

But I accept that you have always had my best interests at heart, so I bear no hard feelings. I for one do not wish to throw myself in front of the 'karma bus'. So, I take this opportunity to acknowledge your good work and express my gratitude for all of the lessons and all of the blessings I have had in my life so far.

Rest assured that I have received all of your messages loud and clear, and even if I wasn't aware of what you were trying to tell me at the time, I think I get it now. I have done a lot of work to become more aware and more conscious.

Universe, it's now time to draw a line in the sand. I don't mean to sound ungrateful; I am extremely grateful for what has been a great life so far, but I haven't quite reached my potential, have I? You have intentionally kept moving the goalposts, so that each time I think I have finally arrived, I find that the rules have changed. I know now that all of this was to make me grow and to make me a better person. I have no regrets; it was all part of my story. Obviously, I wasn't quite ready until now.

Until now, I have been guided by you, but now it's my turn to do the talking, and I really want you to listen. It's time for me to tell you what I want.

The lessons so far have brought me here, and I know it is all for good reason. So from here, this now becomes my platform, the base for everything that comes next. I am not looking back, only forward, but looking forward is only for the purpose of having a vision. I know how important it is to stay in the present. I am well aware that life cannot be measured as a straight line, but rather is made up of a series of dots which together make up the diagram of life.

What I want is to be shown the path which leads me to fulfilling my purpose. I don't think my purpose is a destination as such; perhaps it is more about the things I need to do every day. I can't see a time when everything is done and I get to sit back and admire the view. I believe my purpose needs to be worked on every single day, and if I am grateful for every single step along the way, I won't need to wait to experience the rewards, the rewards will come every day, along the way.

So, Universe, what I am looking for is alignment: alignment to the things that are best for me, the things I deserve, the things I am worthy of. I am not willing to lower my frequency. The things and the people who are meant to be on my journey will be sitting there alongside me on my wavelength. Help me to recognise these when I encounter them and to make the most of these encounters.

This is my time; I hope you agree. I have been patient. I have recognised the signs you put out in front of me. I have agreed to deviate from the course so I could learn the lessons properly. I'm not saying that I don't have a lot more to learn, but I promise I will be more compliant and aware, so we don't have to repeat the same boring lessons again. I get it! I got it!

Please bring me into alignment and on the path to realising my fullest potential and being the best person I can possibly be; firstly, to myself, then to my family, and to all of those I encounter on my path, particularly those who take the time to connect and nourish my soul.

Universe, thank you for showing me that in the absence of fear I can accomplish great things. I am responsible for my own happiness and the only person I am accountable to is me. I know, it took me a long time to get here.

I am here now, ready for what you throw my way next. My coordination is not great, so I can't promise I will always catch it the first time, but what I lack in physical skill, I make up for in creativity.

So, Universe, I hope you understand that from now on I'm going to be a little more demanding. Just putting it out there so the both of us are under no illusion as to where we stand. I'm calling the shots now, you've had your turn, now it's mine.

Kind regards

Pina

WHY?

I believe the answer to most things lies in one simple question: *Why?* So, why did I start writing books?

I write them for me. It's my way of documenting how I feel about certain things so I can make sense of them and reconcile those thoughts in my mind. My mind is just so full of stuff sometimes that it literally takes a download to unpack all of the ideas and put them into some reasonable order.

The journey started around my 40th birthday, when suddenly everything I thought to be true was brought under the microscope and put into question. It was time to clean up the mess and prepare to move through the next phase a little lighter and with a higher purpose. This phase of gradual awakening, trials, tests and tribulations, wasn't always much fun, but in retrospect, I am grateful for the lessons I have learnt. As I look back over that time, I can clearly see how the Universe was trying to shift me to a better place.

But boy, did I put up a fight at times. I am definitely a stubborn one! I can just picture the Universe rolling her eyes every time I resisted.

I can hear it now:

> Guides: Houston, we have a problem. This one is a live wire; she just won't put her trust in us.
>
> Universe: Not again! Oh well, we're just going to have to keep working on her until she comes around. We may have to take the lesson up a notch!

In the end, she proved she was stronger than me, and I had to give in and realise that I was the student and she was the teacher.

Although I had to repeat some of the lessons numerous times, I finally got there in the end. And sure, some are still a work in progress. But I am grateful that all of the lessons to this point have been achieved without too much damage being done. I am well aware that if I don't get the message in time, the lessons will become more testing—and I for one would rather avoid that at all costs.

As I said earlier, my writing was primarily for me. But once I shared the themes with some of my closest friends, I discovered that they did indeed resonate with others.

I discovered that each of us, in our own unique way, does go through the same sorts of things throughout the various stages of our lives. The writing then became something I could possibly share with others as a means of inspiring and motivating them to rise above all the crap and view things from a different perspective.

There have been many times in my life when I have felt that nobody wanted to listen to me. Like the language I was speaking was different to everyone else's. I have always been the tough one, the strong one. So independent was I that nobody ever bothered to ask how I was doing; they still don't! But the strong ones are often the ones that are overlooked, and as a result, they suffer in silence and fall under the radar because nobody expects them to be vulnerable in any way.

I just want everyone out there who feels this way to know that I see them, and I hear them. I know what it feels like when nobody seems to understand where you are coming from. It can really be a lonely place.

I have had to learn some of my lessons the hard way. I had to learn that *I have value* and that *I am worthy*. It took me a while, but eventually I came to realise that *I am enough*, just the way I am. I had to learn that to strive for perfection was the sure way to guarantee failure. What many of us share—and it's not our fault, it's just the way we are conditioned to be—is the feeling that we to have to fit within a particular mould. These moulds have been created for us by society, and while much has changed over time, the moulds have barely had a facelift. If anything, the criteria to fit them have become even more narrow.

What happens when you don't quite fit the mould? Well, I'll tell you. Nobody knows exactly how to handle you. They try to fit you inside a box but it's never really the right fit, you keep spilling out the edges. No matter how hard they try to secure the lid on top of the box, it just doesn't seem to work. But why are they trying to make you fit in when you were clearly born to stand out?

Eventually, the time comes when you begin to question the rules and regulations imposed by society. And when you begin to ask those questions, nobody can really give you a straight answer. That's because there isn't one. When I came to this realisation on my own, I felt I had been robbed of my freedom. My culture had conspired with society to keep me small, and I didn't even realise it was happening. Until the lights came on, that is!

And slowly but surely, I went through a process of cleaning out what no longer served a purpose in my life. From people to ideas to self-imposed limitations. A work in progress, which will inevitably last for some time to come. I had to unlearn quite a few things which I had been brought up to believe. They no longer have a place in my life and should not have a place in future generations.

Who Switched the Lights On? is essentially a book about life—my life—and this one represents the next instalment.

More than self-help books, they document a journey over time which highlights my growth and the things I was able to learn, or unlearn, along the way. It is my hope that by coming along with me as I adjust to the light, clear out the cobwebs, and work through my process of 'un-conditioning', you too will be inspired to shine a light on your own life and adjust the brightness until it's just perfect for you.

It's time to dig deep, grab your torch, put on your sunglasses. We've got work to do.

THE REMAINING COBWEBS

To be totally honest, this was not the book I thought I would be writing. But it makes absolute sense that it is. As I write this book, I am also trying my hand at writing fiction. Writing fiction is new to me. I like to think I write from my soul, so it took me a while to come to grips with the fact that, if I was writing fiction, then I was writing a fabrication. I reconciled this in my mind by knowing that I could still write from my soul if the themes were real and I was inventing the characters to illustrate the learnings. So, this is what I did.

I enjoy immersing myself into the role of each character and having complete power to shape their history, their personality, their choices and therefore their futures—something we are seemingly powerless to do in reality. Or so we think. The characters in my fiction work are not real, but they are the sum total of everything I have read, experienced and watched on television, the people I have encountered and the stories they have shared with me. All of this information is stored in my subconscious, to be drawn out for the purposes of a good read and the delivery of many hidden messages.

But it makes sense for me to follow on from where I left off in *Who Switched the Lights On?*. That part of my story may have reached a suitable ending, but just like everything in life, it ushered in the beginning of a whole new series of chapters. Things were looking much lighter until they abruptly veered off course due to some unexpected shadows cast over my otherwise bright outlook.

I believe I have come a long way, particularly over the last year. I have come to realise a lot about myself, and the social structures we live by. In the process, I have come to challenge some of those structures, and as a result, have had to rewrite for myself some of the narrative around them.

What I have learnt is that it is perfectly okay to change the ending of the story or to change the characters in your book. Our life is based on the story we choose to believe. The story is one we have been told by our ancestors and influenced by the society we are born into. We have no idea who invented these stories, or why. We don't know the intention of the original author; nor do we know the context surrounding the story. But we continue to believe these stories, even though the world around us continues to evolve. Such is the power of these structures that centuries later, we remain stuck in the beliefs of a bygone era.

All around us, we are beginning to see evidence of these structures starting to topple. Our political leaders face challenges that were not written in the textbook. Heads of big business either abandon their position or shut up shop altogether. We begin to see the hypocrisy within the religions that dictate the rules by which we should live, as they turn a blind eye to their own internal failings. And at the time of writing, the US is contending with widespread protesting and looting, triggering similar behaviour in many cities around the world.

People say the system is broken. But it isn't. It is still fulfilling its original purpose. The problem is that we are still conforming to a system that was designed a very long time ago. While humanity has evolved, these systems have not.

I was raised a Catholic but I see the Catholic Church as an example of where failure to evolve can lead to catastrophic results. It is one of the few churches in the world to demand a vow of celibacy. Look at where that has got them. We don't know the intention of God; we only know the interpretation of a book written by a group of people thousands of years ago. It doesn't make any sense to me that God would create man and woman in the way he did, if the only way one could show a true devotion to God was to remain celibate. This goes against the very nature of creation itself.

The label we give to a person does not determine their ability to carry out their purpose. Whether or not a priest or nun takes an oath of celibacy does not affect their ability to do what God wants them to do—that is, to lead by example and spread his word, and most of all to teach people to love one another. I am absolutely certain that the underlying message of all God's work is Love.

It's as simple as that. Do all things with and through love.

Labels and categories are things that society invented, not God. We invented them in order to establish a system of order and a set of laws and standards to live by. We are taught that laws exist to keep us safe and protected. That they are for our benefit. But how does this work in a world where the only constant is change, and the only thing not keeping up with this change is society itself?

The system is not broken; it just doesn't work anymore. It needs to evolve. To quote Albert Einstein, 'Problems can never be solved with the same way of thinking through which they have arisen'.

And I think that is absolutely correct.

Much as I hate to question why certain things happen to me, I find myself doing it anyway. It makes me feel most ungrateful because I know too well that the challenges I face can be overcome. Many people out there are facing challenges that have absolutely no solution or chance of being resolved. So, every time I find myself feeling sorry for myself, I can hear how ungrateful and childish I sound, so I quickly cancel out that thought.

Yes, I am scared of karma. Aren't you? I am scared of bad karma, that is. I am a big believer that you get in life what you give. I forget sometimes, and I find myself in a cycle of negativity, but eventually I come back to a space of acceptance and gratitude, which is the karma I prefer to have returned to me.

Lately, I find myself feeling very tired. Tired of the lessons, the continual setbacks, the days when I can't remember what I am supposed to do. I find it very difficult to exist when I don't have a clear view of where I am going. In saying that, I am not attached to an outcome and nor do I need assurances of what I get when I arrive. I know full well that life is about the process of being the best you can be every single day and not so much about actually arriving anywhere. I just need to see that I am on a road where I have a purpose and am being fulfilled along the way. Sometimes, I need just a little sign that I am on the right path.

But as I am continuously reminded: believe it and you will see it, as opposed to believe it when you see it. This is what it means to have real faith. To trust in something greater than yourself because there is a part of you, deep down inside, that knows exactly when the path you are on is the right one. The confirmation of it being the right path is that there is no resistance; everything comes easy and effortlessly. It's called alignment.

When you bring into alignment what you know in your soul to be true and the path it takes to get there, success is guaranteed. When things work out positively, we have a tendency to refer to it as luck, when in fact it is alignment. Alignment is the key to achieving everything that resides within your soul. Once you reach the point where you are aligned, it all makes complete sense and gives you a great deal of happiness because this is what you signed up for. But as a human being, you are just not conscious of the fact you did.

There are examples of people doing good all around us. People who are following their passion and achieving much success and happiness in the process. When things are not looking too great for us, it's easy to look over at the neighbour and think 'Boy, aren't they lucky'. But once again, achievement is about alignment not luck. The things that come into our lives are the things that we are aligned to. We are all tuned into a frequency. This is where we get our vibe from. A low and negative vibe will only attract more of the same, so it makes sense that a higher vibe puts you in a better position to achieve greater things.

So next time you feel like you're down on your luck (and let's face it, we all feel this way at times), look at it instead in terms of alignment. Adjust your vibe to the level of frequency that aligns with your soul, and there you have it. Boom! Magic!

What I have learnt is that in order to evolve you must continue to grow and learn. You must shed the limitations that hold you back. Many of these are self-imposed due to us believing in the stories told to us by those around us. It's not their fault really. They have been fed a similar story in their history too. And if you do not challenge those narratives, I am afraid that you too will continue to pass those stories down the line to those who come after you, unless you break those generational patterns. That is, only if you want to, of course.

I can see very clearly that I am now repeating the lessons that I have not yet mastered. The big one for me, and I am sure many of you will relate to this, is the feeling of not being worthy, of not being enough: good enough, smart enough, pretty enough, and the list goes on. In the business context, it is usually referred to as the 'imposter syndrome'. This one is a big one for most of us and I believe it goes to the heart of humanity. Commercialisation relies on us not believing we are enough. We therefore look for things external to ourselves to fill that void. We will accumulate and experiment with things to make us feel better, until we eventually discover that the only thing that will make us feel better has been inside us all along. And we spent all that time and money looking for something we already had.

This particular lesson seems to keep coming back to me in many different forms. At times, just when I think I have mastered it, I am delivered another dose, just to make sure. Obviously, I continue to fall short of being completely cured. It keeps coming back because it must be a prerequisite for moving to the next level of my evolution. Sometimes I wonder if it would be easier to crawl back into my cocoon, where I was asleep and not so conscious of the things around me. Like I said, it can be quite comfortable and cosy in the dark, when you are oblivious to the light outside.

But as we are well aware, movement and growth are a forward process. It's a long road and we all need fuel for the ride. My fuel is the knowledge that I am aligned with my purpose and I am heading in the right direction. I am okay with a few twists and turns along the way, a few stops, and even a few strategically placed temptations or choices to be made, only if it is for my higher good, and for that of those closest to me.

MANY SHADES OF LIGHT

Isn't it interesting how we tend to associate the new with the good, and the old with something to leave behind? For me *new* equals *promising*; whether it is good or bad remains a question to be answered in time.

The year 2019 came and went in the blink of an eye, as do most years these days. The year of completion. The end of another decade. True to form, it was indeed the year many things came to an end. Things changed all around me. Some things left; new things came in. Surprisingly, I was okay with it all, even though some of the things leaving my life were of great significance. If I could sum up 2019 in just a few words, it would have to be simultaneously one of best and worst years of my life. Bizarre, but true. Looking forward to 2020, it was an opportunity for a fresh start. The new decade held such promise. Armed with a positive outlook and my attractive new yearly planner, I was prepared for what the new year would bring. Or was I?

Turns out that none of us were. If I look back now, the ringing in of the new year was more like an annoying hum than a joyful tune. Was this the first clue? Perhaps it was, because it has been pretty much downhill since then. Sounding rather negative, I know! What I also know is that there is a silver lining to everything, and sometimes we just have to look a little harder to find it. I'm looking. I am literally turning my world upside down in the hope of finding it.

As much as I like to project a positive persona, I am not feeling very positive at the moment, and I would not be true to myself if I wasn't prepared to admit that. What is it that I have to feel negative about? Possibly nothing, but I can't deny that's how I am feeling. It's fair to say that I have spent the past few days in a relatively dark space. From time to time, a little light filters in. I can see it and its warmth tries to comfort me, but it's not strong enough, just yet, to entice me towards it. I am quite comfortable in the dark for now. Sure, it's cold, but I am getting used to it. I know I can't stay here for very long and I am not quite sure how I am going to get out. But until I am ready to make that choice, I am prepared to sit in this space.

This space is trying to tell me that perhaps I am looking at everything in the wrong way. That the choices I have made recently may have been misguided and perhaps a little selfish. Deep down, I know this is not true, but until I start to believe that wholeheartedly, these are the feelings I am confronted with.

So, let me look at the facts for a minute. Let me take a more practical approach as opposed to my usual 'trust in the universe' approach. If I look at the evidence before me, it appears to support the belief that I may in fact have everything around the wrong way. Currently, I am sitting at home. My home life has been affected by my choices. My choices have made the lives of the ones I love a little more difficult. I chose this path based on the need for me to be true to myself and all I have caused is discord. This was supposed to make me happier, and although it appeared that way for a while, lately there is very little light to be seen on the horizon. Instead of being happier, I find myself feeling quite down.

Every time I articulate something of the nature of what I have just written above, I can hear the answers being thrown right back at me. Either the answers are coming from a place deep within me—my gut, my intuition, or my soul perhaps—or it is the voice of my life coach I am tuning in to.

Either way, I know that what I am saying contradicts everything I have been awakened to. I know it contradicts all the laws of the universe and how things work. If that were true, was I prepared to throw everything I have learnt out the window?

But still, I manage to keep reverting to this space when things get dark. I keep reverting to my old self. And so, as the law states, I will continue to repeat the lesson until I can cross it off the list as being complete. This one is a particularly hard one. I am finding it challenging to master. But I know I must.

In spiritual terms, I believe it is referred to as the 'dark night of the soul'. And while it sounds dark, and it is, it is also an essential part of the growth purpose. As Brené Brown says in her book, *Daring Greatly: How the Courage to Be Vulnerable Transforms the Way We Live, Love, Parent, and Lead*, 'Only when we are brave enough to explore the darkness will we discover the infinite power of the light.'

Those dark moments present us with an opportunity to stare our fears right in the face and deal with them there and then, and hopefully triumph in defeat. It's a time when you need to dig deeper than usual to arrive at the answers. It's sink-or-swim time. You get to choose.

I am trying my hardest to dig deep to get out of this big black hole. Sometimes I fear that I am allowing myself to be drawn further in. I also know that there is a point from which it will be harder to return. So, it is important to keep my wits about me. What I am cognisant of, though, is that it is a choice that I am making to stay in this dark place. I started to think that I couldn't get out of it, before I realised that if I wanted to, I really could. The fact is that I didn't want to. Not just yet anyway.

What made me drop the ball and venture into this space? I believe the challenges that have come my way over the past few months have been the cause of it. The first couple weren't too bad. They were dealt with and I moved on. But they kept coming and it overwhelmed me. It highlighted the fact that they were more serious than I first thought and passing the test would be critical. When they keep coming, you start questioning why they are happening and why you can't seem to cop a break. Then you veer off down a different path.

However, when I put all of these things into perspective and climb up high enough to view it all from that vantage point, I realise they are all things that can indeed be overcome. I just have to choose to overcome them. I know I have the tools to do this because I have learnt to do it. I don't always *use* the tools I have. Sometimes I feel like I have misplaced them, or they are just too heavy to handle when the strength doesn't appear to be there. But I know I have them, somewhere.

When I am too stubborn to dig deep for the right tools, I may come across a shovel and use it to dig the hole instead. Sometimes I just stand at the edge of that big black hole and take a peek inside. I can see what's in there, but I am quite happy to view it from a distance. I can manage to stay where it's safe. Other times, I jump in. I don't go very far. I just venture into the shadows a little bit. I take a look at what I can see in those shadows and try to make sense of it. How quickly I learn the lessons determines how quickly I turn around and venture out of the hole. I know how to get out because I left a trail on the way in.

And sometimes, I allow myself to go even further down into the hole. I even make myself comfortable. I have a little lie down. Hey, sometimes I even come across some of my old stuff that I thought I had buried down there, only to find I hadn't actually done the job properly. Once I see these things, I have no choice but to confront them again, just like Groundhog Day. That usually means I have to stay a little while longer to deal with it all.

From that big black hole, I can hear my friends shouting at me from the top, peering in, trying to find where I've gone.

> My friends: Why don't you come out? Its dark and cold in there. Come back to where it's warm.
>
> Me: I'm okay. I just want to stay down here for a while where its comfortable (and I can feel sorry for myself). I am not alone. I have some friends with me. Anxiety has come in to pay a visit and so has Fear. Unworthiness is giving me a bit of a hard time but I am trying to put her in her place. Guilt and Shame have wandered in too. These guys all tend to hang around together. I need to have a chat with them. They really want to stay but I'm not sure there's enough room for all of us. Once I deal with them, I will send them on their way.

Perhaps the whole purpose of my exploring this space is so that I can write about how it feels, because, let's face it, without the people and experiences in our lives to provide the context, we wouldn't really have anything to write about, would we?

Writing down my thoughts helps me a lot, as it can get very crowded in my mind. Dumping stuff makes room for other stuff to come in, hopefully things of a more positive nature. I don't like clutter in any of my spaces. I like peace and order and I like to know where everything is. Writing helps me to make neat little piles of related themes. It also allows me to understand what I am thinking at times when I really don't know what that is until I see it written down.

As Virginia Woolf said, 'I like to have space to spread my mind out in.'[1]

Rewind back to 1 January. Come to think of it, it did have an unsettled air about it. Like something hanging, suspended. Like something looming. And one was right to think it. Much of Australia was being threatened by bushfires. Unrelenting and without mercy, they took the lives of people and animals, and devastated homes and land. They destroyed businesses and the livelihood of many families, particularly those living in more remote or rural areas.

This tragedy took the lives of at least 22 people, destroyed more than 1500 homes and affected over 12 million hectares of land and killed more than 1 billion animals, many of them native wildlife.[2] It will go down in history as one of Australia's darkest times. The light, however, came in the form of an outpouring of grief and financial support from all around the world.

It took time for the smoke to clear. Parts of the country were blanketed in smoke for weeks on end. A lingering reminder of the power and fury of Mother Nature. With the threat hanging over our heads, questions were raised, and people were held to account for past decisions made. Decisions which only served to fuel the flames. Lessons learnt; we hope.

Still not content, Mother Nature unleashed her fury a few weeks later with vicious storms, causing floods. Properties suffered significant damage and we were reminded of the extremes of nature and how powerless we were to control them.

While so many things were happening for us domestically, there was another storm brewing in another part of the world. And this one was not targeting a particular place on earth, it was targeting the entire earth, and would impact the human race directly.

We have all watched the big Hollywood blockbusters. You know the ones. Doomsday is looming. The government keeps it under wraps to control the panic. There is a hint of a possible conspiracy at the highest level. There are bad guys. And there are good guys who frantically try to solve the problem. And there is the hero, prepared to put his or her life on the line to save the entire human species.

And who would have thought that we would all be cast to play a role in this particular movie? What seemed like something you would only see on the big screen has quickly become our reality, and as I write, this is as real as it gets.

WHEN TIME STOOD STILL

Every day that passes is another day in history. Most days are relatively uneventful as we go about our own business, adding to our own personal histories. Some days are marked by significant events which touch more people, but they too come and go. Then there are days which have the effect of changing the world forever, events of such importance that they are carved in time as moments that shaped humanity.

One that comes easily to mind are the events of 11 September 2001. On this day, the world stood still and watched in complete disbelief as terror was unleashed on New York, causing the destruction of the World Trade Center towers and the loss of 2996 lives.[3] As I sat, glued to my living room chair, watching in utter horror as the images played over and over on the television screen, I held my six-month-old baby ever so tightly. What I knew for sure was that the world he would grow up in would not be the same safe world that I knew as a child.

There is no doubt that 9/11 has been imprinted into the calendar so deep that people will never forget where they were on that day, and how they came to hear the news. And although we were all affected by that event in some way—and by everything that came after this day—for most of us, we were affected from a distance. But still, that effect was profound and the world as we knew it changed forever on that day.

While much of the world came to a grinding halt on that day back in 2001, the actions that followed were swift and decisive, even though the result was a war that killed and scarred many American and allied soldiers, and inevitably destroyed the lives of many who were caught in the crossfire. Although it was a world issue, this event was still quite contained and did not have the power to impact every human life on the planet.

It took a virus to do that. In the year 2020, everyone on this earth gets to take part in yet another significant time in history. Should we consider ourselves fortunate? It seems that very few of us alive today have ever lived through something like this. Why us? And why now?

One of the best quotes I have read in recent months is this one:

World: There's no way we can shut everything down in order to lower emissions, slow climate change and protect the environment.

Mother Nature: Here's a virus. Practise.

She's done it again. We have been warned many times. But we didn't listen. Now we have no choice.

But perhaps this is yet another lesson. It will be interesting to see how much we have learnt from this experience once life returns to normal. Whatever 'normal' means these days. Mother Nature decided the earth needed to heal, so she sent us a challenge that no-one would have expected. A flu-like virus with no vaccine. A virus so powerful that it has basically shut down the world. A concept that until now was inconceivable.

But it just goes to show that there is no such word as *can't*. The more appropriate word is *won't*. The reason why we think we can't is that no-one is prepared to make the sacrifices that it will take. As a society, we have become accustomed to having what we want, when we want it. We have come so far in our evolution that to go back to basics is an extreme stretch that no-one is prepared to make—until we have absolutely no choice, that is.

When someone holds a gun to your head, the threat becomes real, and you have to get creative in order to survive. And then all the things you thought were impossible suddenly become plausible.

And the world came to a standstill.

Planes were grounded.
Borders were closed.
Restaurants were shut down.
Beaches and landmarks became no-go zones.
Retail commerce came to a standstill, only after the panic buying ceased.
Many lost their jobs, causing the economy to falter.
There were fewer cars on the road; petrol became cheap.
People went into their houses and stayed there until they were told it was safe to come out.
Families got to know each other again. They played games and cooked meals together.
Dads played with their children in the parks, at all hours of the day.
Children went outside to play with other children, on bikes, rollerskates and skateboards.
People stopped rushing around with their eyes closed.
Forests regenerated.
The grass became greener.
The skies became a more radiant shade of blue.
People learnt to live with the basics and value the important things.
They found new ways to connect.

And eventually the supermarket shelves were restocked with toilet paper. Yes, a bizarre consequence of this pandemic was that the first thing Australians thought of was that they could not risk running out of toilet paper. It seems that we have in fact been successful in averting that particular disaster. If only our other problems could be sorted out just as easily.

The past couple of months have blended together in a complete blur of nothingness. No idea of the time of day, the day of the week, or the month of the year; it may as well be written off the calendar completely. But at the same time, it is a significant time in history. A time when we were forced to make significant changes to the way we live and learn to value the important things in our lives just a little more.

It will go down in history as a time when humans slowed down to rest, when the earth had the opportunity to heal, where the average person became a national hero, where people looked out for one another, and there was a greater appreciation for the simpler things in life.

It was a time when 'how are you?' was a genuine question and we cared about the response. When we told each other to stay safe and we each did our part to ensure we did. When we kept a watchful eye on our neighbours.

We are all heroes in the story of when time stood still. From the children who undertook their schooling from home, to the teachers who provided the continuity of their education. From parents who worked from home so they could be near their children, to those who had to learn quickly to become teachers. From the delivery people who kept us connected, to those who continued to manufacture our food and keep our supply chains in operation. And let's give a standing ovation to all of the frontline medical staff and defence force personnel who worked tirelessly to protect our community, and to the people charged with leading and guiding us through these challenging times. Every single person has had their part to play, and in this story, every person is a hero.

It still baffles me, however, that this virus—a flu-like virus, like the many different strains of influenza we see each year—has had the ability to shut the world down. The threat of this virus was so bad that we were willing to sacrifice our economy in order to reduce its spread. Just like in the Hollywood movies, compounded by my conspiracy tendencies, there is still some part of the puzzle that I feel we may be missing.

With no idea of which day it is, it really does feel like we are living in the twilight zone. I am getting very used to wearing activewear, even when I am not being very active. Gone are the days of getting dressed up for work. What even are high heels, anyway? And make-up? Well … it has been a while. The occasional online Zoom meeting may require just a little more effort from the waist up, but all in all, the ugg boots have become my favourite footwear, cementing their place underneath the desk.

What have we lost? We have lost all of the expectation. And that, in my eyes, is a good thing.

Suddenly, there is no expectation to be anywhere, do anything, be available whenever you are called on, be dressed in a certain way, look a certain way, do or be a certain thing. We are all just expected to do our best. That is where expectation begins and ends. Oh, and washing your hands, and keeping a safe physical distance. This is expected. We have become extremely educated on all of those important things. Who would have thought that one of the greatest lessons to come from a pandemic is that humanity finally learnt how to wash their hands properly?

And the buzzword of 2020 is … 'social distancing'. Now, I wonder which bright spark in the world coined that particular phrase. We are already a disconnected bunch. Social interactions and connections are important to our wellbeing. What's wrong with calling it what it is, 'physical distancing'? We need to pay more attention to our choice of words. Keeping it simple makes it easier to understand what we are required to do.

In the past few days, we have been told that we are now ready to go back into the real world, in stages. As we open back up for business, I find myself feeling a little apprehensive. I have become quite comfortable hibernating in my little cocoon. I am not sure I want to emerge just yet. I'm not really feeling like a butterfly and considering it has been some time since I visited the hairdresser and the beautician, I am not exactly looking like one either. But just as we adjusted to the shutdown, we will adjust and re-emerge into the real world.

But there seems to be an invisible line in the sand, with pre-covid-19 and post-covid-19 on either side. Are we the same as who we were before this all started? Who are we now? It's wonderful that we have now been educated on how to wash our hands properly, but the distancing still needs to be maintained. What does this mean for our society? Will we just get used to the idea and seek to maintain our own personal space? No hugging, no kissing, no handshakes. My goodness, what will all my Italian friends do?

In a previous life, I used to rush around like a mad woman, always needing to be somewhere by a certain time. Always trying to fit everything into the limited hours in the day. Was I ever present like I am today? When I don't really need to be anywhere. When there is no expectation other than to look after yourself. Everything is flexible. Look at the ways we have worked to get through this. I am not sure I can go back to how things were. I am not even sure I want to.

Humanity has found new ways to connect, and some of these new ways are likely to stay. We have had to be creative with very few resources and I am pleased to say that it appears we have passed the test. The resilience and patience shown over the past few months, the collaboration of our leaders, and the focus on working together for the greater good has been inspiring and gives us hope that we have in fact learnt some valuable lessons.

The earth has done its fair share of healing during this shutdown. It is reported that the canals of Venice are the clearest they have ever been. That the skies over countries with heavy pollution are now looking cleaner. That the hole in the ozone layer has started to repair itself. We take for granted the harm we do to the earth as we exploit its resources. Maybe the earth was not intended to be used in the way to which we have become accustomed. Will this experience teach us all to value our natural resources more than we currently do? Perhaps we need to find a way to give back some of what we take out.

Is this slow down the reset we all needed?

Once again, all will be revealed in time.

THE 'D' WORD

Let me tell you a little story. It's one you may have heard before.

> There once was a little girl who lived in a nice house with her family. She loved to play in her cubbyhouse and dream of her future. She also loved books, particularly those with a happy ending. She too, dreamt that one day she would meet her Prince Charming. He would be handsome and loving. He would think she was the most beautiful girl in the world. He would whisk her away on his white horse and declare his undying love for her.
>
> They would get married. She would wear the most exquisite wedding gown. There would be flowers and music and happy people everywhere. Everyone would rejoice and the girl and her prince would live happily ever after.

You've heard this one before, right? There are many variations of this story, and today, there are many different aspects of what constitutes a committed relationship, and between whom. But the outcome of this traditional and most widely told story is always the same. Boy meets girl. They fall in love. They get married. They live happily ever after. End of story.

But nobody tells you about the things that happens in between. It seems that almost every girl dreams of getting married someday. Synonymous with the word 'marriage' seems to be the word 'forever'. In the last chapter we talked about expectation. This is another one of those expectations sitting beneath the stories we are led to believe.

So, is the dream more about the wedding than the actual marriage? As young girls we dream about what the day would look like. I certainly did. I had every single detail illustrated in my mind, in the virtual scrapbook that lay within my subconscious. No expense would be spared in planning the perfect day. As if this would have any impact on the life that lay ahead.

The perfect day does not result in the perfect marriage. And just a reminder right here: there is no such thing as the perfect marriage. And if anyone tells you their marriage is without its challenges, either internal or external, then they are most likely lying.

Marriage is hard work and it goes through its own life cycle. The good, the bad and the ugly. The many things sent to test it: financial considerations and those little humans that come into your life, stealing your attention and so needy of your time. It takes a great deal of resilience to weather the storms that a couple will inevitably face. How else would a relationship grow if it too were not tested from time to time?

And once again, our friend luck enters into our conversation. Many would consider those in a long and successful marriage to be the lucky ones. The ones that were blessed in the marriage sweepstakes and were able to draw their perfect match. But we know that it is not about luck at all; once again, it is about alignment.

When you meet your mate there is something in your energy that draws you to one another. For some, that magnetic pull is stronger than it is for others. Whether or not this is your soulmate, your twin flame, or just the person who you need in your life at that particular point in time, it is all about alignment with that person's energy. The frequency on which you vibrate will draw to you a mate who is on a similar frequency to you. It is the alignment of the two souls and divine timing which bring about the union.

Throughout the relationship, the two people continue to evolve individually, quite independently of the other, even though most feel that you grow as a couple. You don't. Your relationship as a couple may grow, but this is separate from the individuals. Each individual must travel his or her own path. Each will have their own unique purpose. Each person is responsible for their own happiness.

To successfully continue on the journey of marriage requires many different things, but once again it depends on alignment. Is there enough space and respect for each person to continue to be their individual self? As each individual grows, to some extent, they need to grow at a similar rate in order to maintain that all-important alignment which keeps them travelling on the same frequency. It is when the relationship is no longer in alignment that the cracks start to appear, and like everything else in life, if it is no longer the thing that serves you, it will start to make its way out of your life.

For many reasons, many tend to resist these changes. Either they turn a blind eye to them, or they become so preoccupied with other things, such as their children and their work lives, that they start to neglect the relationship or choose to ignore the warning signs in order to avoid the need to confront the issues.

After all, marriage is supposed to be forever, right? Isn't that how the story goes?

It took some time for me to become aware that my marriage was not perfect. And when I did become aware of it, it took me even longer to admit it to myself. I was one of those people who believed the story and was committed to the concept of forever: 'until death do us part'.

I believed that I had indeed found my soulmate. The person who understood me better than anyone else, who shared the same values. Someone I could grow with. But even in writing this, I do recall that I didn't really believe in fairy tales as much as I wanted to. I had a very realistic side to me. And if I look back now, with the wisdom and benefit of hindsight, perhaps I could have predicted the ending of this particular story.

Do I regret any of it? Absolutely not! I have the utmost respect for the father of my children. He is a wonderful man and a great father. We had a very good life together. So what changed, you ask? It was all a question of falling out of alignment.

Society demands a concrete reason for a marriage breakdown. Acceptable reasons include adultery and domestic violence. Death is also an acceptable end to a relationship. But to decide that two people have failed to grow at the same rate, that they are on very different and unrelated paths, and that the marriage is no longer sustainable, is a difficult pill for most to swallow.

Society has created yet another set of rules that we hesitate to break because the feelings of guilt and shame are much too great for us to bare. How do we explain or rationalise a decision to sever a relationship which was supposed to be capable of overcoming difficulties and of weathering every storm?

The fact is that people change and grow, and on the other hand some don't. Things were not so bad for me, but was I completely happy? Not always. Much of the time, I was merely existing. Is it another person's fault if I was not happy? No, it isn't. It is mine, and only mine. And that is why I ultimately had to make a choice. It was not enough for me to merely exist when I believed I deserved to be fulfilled. And now, I am not in search of happiness with someone else, but to have happiness and peace within myself.

I don't completely understand how some people jump out of a relationship and into a new one right away. I am not saying that another 'right' person can't come across your path. The timing of it is not entirely in your control. But taking the time to get to know yourself and to piece yourself back together as a whole person before heading into another relationship will put you in a better position to enjoy a more fulfilling relationship.

Sometimes in life, we have to accept that not everything goes according to our plans. When we enter into an agreement such as marriage, we are bound by a set of vows which are loosely defined to say the least. At the time of entering into the agreement, we believe and hope it will be forever. But what this particular contract doesn't factor in is the needs of both parties, the handling of disputes, the room for personal development, and the constant need to check in and see if the parties are meeting the terms of the agreement.

Who in their right minds would sign a contract so vague, without reading the fine print or seeking legal advice before they do so? But we do it anyway. We sign ourselves up for life based on our faith and based on what we believe is expected of us in the natural progression of our lives.

Marriage is a wonderful institution. But it is an institution. Once you enter into it, you are expected to stay there until the end. There is absolutely nothing wrong with that, provided that within that institution, you have everything you need to grow as individuals and as a unit, and where the love is not conditional on any one thing. It is this that provides the strength for us to deal with obstacles that may get in the way.

When things go pear-shaped there is a tendency to blame it on things or people that have changed. But just as my youngest daughter so eloquently put it to me one day, 'there is a big difference between changing and growing, growing is a positive thing'. Right at that moment, I felt another light bulb switch on in my mind. And for all the words in the world, I couldn't have said it any better myself.

Growth is a prerequisite for learning and working towards the fulfilment of your purpose. It is natural that not all of us grow at exactly the same rate. Even though your particular story may not play out according to the script we are all accustomed to, it is still possible to get your happy ending. The beauty of being the author of your own story, or the architect of your own life, is that you can choose to make it look any way you desire.

That is well within your power.

IRONICALLY SPEAKING

There is so much irony hiding in amongst everything these days.

Initially, the title that came to me for this book was *It's Getting Brighter Now*. What I have written so far leans more towards the dark than the light. So I am beginning to question why that title even came to me at all. I am not ready to write it off just yet, because it probably is just another one of those tricks from the Universe, making me dig a little deeper to rediscover the light that was switched on years ago and has been flickering and gaining strength ever since.

Now that you are reading this book, you will note that the title is different from the one I initially came up with. And although I tried hard to commit to that title, I realised that however hopeful I was about things getting brighter, as each day of this very interesting year passed, it just wasn't getting bright enough to justify the title. The more I wrote, the more it became apparent that the world has become quite a dark place, and while there is always light at the end of a dark tunnel, for the moment, none of us have any idea how long the tunnel is, not even the experts.

Forever the optimist, I am not willing to close the door on things turning around once we have gone through this reset. Way beyond the horizon, the clouds will eventually prepare to lift, exposing the bright warm rays of the sun, once again. And who knows, perhaps I can reserve my original title for much more pleasant days in the future.

Since I wrote my last book, I have been asked the question, 'Who did switch the lights on?' Simple question, right? Makes complete sense that someone would ask that. And why had I never ever thought that it would be the one which would be most asked of me?

As I reflected, I came to realise that I was the one asking the question of who switched the lights on. And that question was based on the assumption that there must have been an external force who had switched the lights on for me. Some supreme being, or superpower, had decided that I was ready to see things that I had never seen before. But no, as much as I would like to believe in superheroes, it was actually me who switched them on. And those light switches, they were not external switches. They were ones I had within me all along.

It was me who switched the lights on. I chose to find the light within me. I had to search to find that light because it was dark all around me. I looked everywhere for some guidance and hope until I realised that it all rested with me. The cause and the solution, the answers, were all within me. The last couple of months have been a little dim, I must admit. But because I know how warm the light is, I am drawn to finding it. I have perhaps allowed my light to be extinguished a little by the forces around me. I can play the victim and blame others for this relapse, but the truth is that once again, the solutions reside in the choices we make, and we all individually have those choices available to us at all times.

It is all a matter of perspective. Making the necessary changes often involves a rewriting of the narrative and taking the time to adjust to the changes. It doesn't happen overnight. Once again, it is a process. And the only way to get to the other side is to go *through* it.

A friend of mine made a very important point. When I found myself referring to different aspects of my life as quiet, or boring, or challenging, she said 'Try adding the words "at the moment" to the end of each of those sentences'. It changes their meaning altogether. Go on, try it! You will find it becomes a little more temporary, more fluid, and just a little easier to deal with. Not as stuck and rigid.

In the end, life is just a series of moments. Nothing is ever set in concrete.

The past few months have shown us that everything in life is temporary. In the face of this current pandemic, we have come to realise that plans can be interrupted, that nothing is certain, that things can be taken away from us at a moment's notice, and that the only thing that matters is our health and that of those around us.

We have also been shown how everything in life is connected. How the effect on one thing can cause another thing to be affected, and how these effects expand and grow exponentially, much like the virus itself.

It has taken a virus to shake us to our core. It has taken a virus to force us to be creative, to find new and inventive ways of doing things. It has taken a virus to bring even the world's strongest economies to their knees. We are all at the mercy of something we can't see, touch or fight. If this doesn't put things into perspective, I don't hold out much hope for the future of humanity.

In my last book, I wrote a whole chapter on my beloved dog. That makes me sound like I am a lover of animals, doesn't it? And while I can't say that I have always been fond of them, perhaps now I do in fact love them. I can attribute that learning to the very best and most loving animal I know. The point of that particular chapter was to highlight the unconditional love of animals towards their owners, as well as the way they are just present. Living in the moment.

Sadly, we were recently forced to say goodbye to our beloved pooch Nacho. Although we knew the day would eventually come, and we often considered it with complete and utter dread, we would never have thought that day would come when it did. And the pain of losing him is like losing a best friend or a member of the family.

What started out as an ordinary day quickly spiralled into a significant day for all of the wrong reasons. The energy of that day was different, and one to remember. It was a beautiful sunny day, uncharacteristically so for mid-May. The last I saw of Nacho in a conscious state was when he was sitting in the back of my car with my daughter, looking a little pensive and wondering where the hell we were going.

We had never been very good at taking Nacho to the vet. We only went when we had a reason to, and he had rarely given us reason. But he had been looking very sad in what were to become his last days. He had lost a significant amount of weight and wasn't eating. There was something about him that was a cause for concern. He would follow me around the house—again, totally out of character—as if he was trying to get my attention, to tell me something.

The sadness in his eyes was unmistakable, and looking back now, I know he must have been in a great deal of pain. But still, there was no trouble, no complaining, almost a complete understanding of his own destiny and an acceptance of what lay ahead.

The prognosis hadn't seemed that bad at first, and as the day went on, many more tests were being carried out. But something deep in my soul knew that there was something different about this particular day. On receiving the initial lot of positive news, I smiled to myself and quietly noted the fact that I have an overactive mind.

But when you know something at a very deep level, you just know it. Exploratory surgery on that same day, expected to be routine, turned out to reveal an inoperable tumour. I knew something was up when I hadn't heard from the vet and it was getting late in the day. Then suddenly my phone rang, and the tone in her voice alone spoke volumes. There was no way out of this, and a decision had to be made.

We were completely devastated. Though it had been nine years, it felt like yesterday that we were drooling over photos from the breeder of this gorgeous pooch, and here we were saying goodbye to our beloved pet who was still under sedation after his surgery. We could have woken him up and kept him with us for a little while longer. But how can you care for an animal who can't openly communicate and who can't tell you it is in pain? It was a difficult decision, but an easy one at the same time.

Anything else would have been selfish on our part, and absolutely cruel to Nacho.

And the very worst part about losing pets is the feeling of guilt, of perhaps not having understood them properly, and of not knowing if they understood what was going on and the reasons why you made particular decisions. Could you have done something to avoid it? You will never know.

I never would have thought that losing a pet would be so painful. When the time comes to say goodbye, parting is inevitable. But to suffer a meaningful loss means that you have loved, and therein lies the blessing in this particular story.

We will never replace or forget our beautiful dog. He really was a rare breed. We are so grateful to have had him in our lives, even if it was for a short time.

As you can see, it's been a little difficult to see the light through the trees lately. I have to write about it so I can see the lessons that come out of every setback. I feel that this time in my life is significant in the whole scheme of things, even though I can't quite pinpoint why.

I can't complain; I don't like to play the victim. These obstacles are all surmountable. I take them as just another dot placed on my history chart. They will pass and I will move onto the next dot.

Like many people around me, I am just having to dig a little deeper to keep the faith. The spotlight is shining on many different elements of my life at the moment, while the Universe moves around the pieces on its chessboard to create the perfect scenario, in preparation for me to face the next battle.

Oh, you didn't think it was over yet, did you?

TWILIGHT ZONE— SEASON 2

Halfway through a year that feels very much like we are trapped in a game of Jumanji. Every month that passes is hopefully a step closer to whatever is at the opposite end of the tunnel. The Melbourne winter has finally set in, but today is pleasantly bright and sunny.

Time to enter the ring for the next round. We are locking down for season 2.0. Definitely sounds like we have contracted a virus, in more ways than you can even begin to imagine. What is it with the year 2020? We can't seem to cop a break! And it appears the world has gone completely mad. We had been doing quite well until now, and suddenly it seems that we have dropped the ball. People are starting to rebel and to ask questions. The problem, however, is in the way these questions are being asked. It is creating a great deal of drama and unrest.

Where people once seemed to be compliant, mainly during the first iteration of lockdown, it now seems they are reverting to their former selves. And it is this complacency and unwillingness to follow guidelines that is causing us our current issues. At times, it feels almost like the start of an uprising. Not that I know what that feels like. My knowledge extends only to things I have read or seen in films. My concern is that anarchy can be just as contagious as a virus. We are currently witnessing the herd mentality at its finest: people following others because something is trending, and not really stopping to ask the right questions, or to ask *why*.

Why would anyone do something if they don't know why they're doing it?

If we are to fully understand something, the context around it and the perspective needs to be clear. If we are unable to see the full picture, or the bigger picture, the choices we make are based on the actions of others and can be misleading because we don't have all the facts. Fear then comes into the equation and all rationality is completely thrown out the window.

It is not my desire to enter into a political debate. I value my life far too much. It feels as though at the moment, there is little respect for an individual's right to have an opinion. Right now, if you don't just move along with the herd, you may just be putting yourself in the line of fire. It seems that nobody wants to listen to the voice of reason.

It's much more interesting to buy into the drama and fear that is being created.

What we fail to consider, however, is that this drama and fear is actually part of a bigger plan; the one of control. By buying into the drama, we are creating a scenario in which we are showing that we are out of control and therefore many of our freedoms should be taken away from us. Look at the evidence. We are being controlled in what we can and can't do. The more we don't follow the rules, the tighter the restrictions being imposed and the higher the penalties for non-compliance.

We are being asked to be tested for a virus, and to download an app which registers where we go and who we come into contact with. Great in theory, and we are told it is in our best interest, but I wonder in the end, whose interest it is really serving. And suddenly no-one is talking about the app anymore. No more advertisements for it. I wonder why.

Yes, it seems I am having a conspiracy theory moment! But as I sit here and observe what it is happening around me, something tells me that there is a part of this picture we are not seeing. It just doesn't all fit with me. The picture is still very much obscured and out of focus. But from a different perspective, it is an interesting human experiment and says a great deal about how humans behave and interact. All I ask is that people take the time to consider the aspects that they are not quite seeing. To ask the right questions and challenge what they are being told, and to take a practical and rational approach based on the real evidence before them.

Just because someone says something, it doesn't mean it is true. To get the answers you need, you have to ask the right questions.

Let me give you a couple of examples and let me try to be politically mindful while doing so. I am only trying to provide context, not commentary. I don't want to see footage of people on the streets burning my book because of something I have written or said.

Despite it appearing as if we had finally won the battle against covid-19, where I live, the relaxing of restrictions and our complacency have in fact led to a second wave. History tell us that the second wave is often more detrimental than the first. The 'Spanish flu' of 1918, considered to be the deadliest epidemic in world history, came in three waves. It is estimated that 500 million people worldwide were infected with the virus, of whom somewhere between 20 and 50 million people died as a result[4]. The number of actual deaths is difficult to ascertain due to lack of medical record keeping, but some estimates have the number of deaths closer to 100 million, or 3 per cent of the population. The first wave of the Spanish flu hit in the spring and was relatively mild, with a low number of casualties. By the following autumn, the second wave hit with a vengeance resulting in the greatest number of casualties. The symptoms were much swifter and people died within days of catching the disease. The third wave came during the summer of 1919. Symptoms were much more moderate as the virus finally began to subside.

We have come a long way since the days of the Spanish flu, and we have a lot more at our disposal now to combat this current pandemic. But despite this, covid-19 has managed to wreak havoc on the world, in particular on our economies and our mental health. So here we go, panic round number two. Supermarket shelves are now starting to look empty again, and many of the businesses that had shut down are unable to continue to sustain such losses. Humans can deal with crises when they are temporary, but the longer they continue, the more we tend to dilute their importance. People stop taking the care that is required in such circumstances.

Each day on the news we see the numbers creep higher, causing the chart to spike once again. When I consider the numbers which, may I add, are resulting in the shutdown of entire suburbs and sending residents into lockdown, it makes sense that the more we test for a particular thing, the more likely we are to find it. This is purely mathematical. We are currently conducting more testing than practically anywhere else in the world. Sure, this is a good thing, but the problem is that we are being scared by the numbers, which we have to expect if we are specifically testing for something.

So my questions are around things that we are not being told in the media to give us context. Namely, what is the condition of people who currently have the virus? What demographic do they fall into? Are they young or old? Do they have any underlying medical conditions? Are any of them being treated in hospital? And what is the treatment for the virus? What is the rate of recovery? Are there any underlying side effects or risk to future health?

The number we focus on most is the number of the 'new cases', when the more important numbers in my eyes are the 'active cases'. Adding new cases is a problem, but there is a greater problem if people are not recovering from the virus. It is the active cases, not just the new ones, that increase the risk of exposure and therefore create the greater threat.

And why is it that nobody is talking about the rates of suicides and the consequences of the increases in domestic violence during this time? I have no doubt that those statistics will be more alarming than the ones we have become accustomed to seeing flashed across our television screens each day. Our society will inevitably pay a hefty price and shoulder a heavy burden as a result of the current circumstances.

Just for the record, there seem to be fewer deaths this year from the ordinary influenza viruses, as most deaths seem to be attributed to covid-19, even those which have been indirectly caused by the virus but where there was a significant underlying primary condition. Measures such as isolation, social distancing and the wearing of masks have significantly impacted the flu statistics for this year.

As a result of these measures the numbers are difficult to interpret.[5] Last year, in 2019, Australia recorded its worst flu season on record, with more than 310 thousand people presenting to hospitals and health services. Of these, 900 people died as a direct result of influenza. This was slightly less than the highest number (1100), which was recorded in 2017.[6]

And while we are talking statistics, over 3000 Australians die from suicide each year, with depression being a significant risk factor. Statistics show that in 2017, 65,000 people attempted suicide,[7] with the suicide rate being more than twice the road toll. In 2018, there were 3046 deaths by suicide,[8] which equates to 8.3 deaths per day. I hate to see what the statistics from this year will tell us. It's a frightening thought.

We don't know the answers to many of our questions, and the media seem to think it is okay to provide only half of the information in order to spread panic. Can the real virus please step forward?

In another part of the world, in the midst of this pandemic, a different type of contagion threatens to spread: that of bad behaviour. Once again, we see people being discriminated against supposedly because of the colour of their skin. In today's day and age, this simply should not happen. There is absolutely no question. I do have one issue though. A man of colour had allegedly committed a crime and the policeman (who happened to be white) did the most unthinkable thing and let the situation spiral out of control, with fatal consequences. This should not have happened, and the policeman should be punished to the full extent of the law. I do not have an issue with any of that.

What I do have an issue with, however, is how this event has infiltrated the entire world. In many parts of the world, it has sparked a debate about racism and discrimination and has been adapted to suit the particular circumstances in each country. This is of course an important conversation. There is absolutely no place for this type of behaviour anywhere, and if we stop putting people into stereotypical categories and drop all of the labels cultivated by our society, we will be left with the common denominator: that every human is equal and is therefore entitled to be treated as such. It is as simple as this.

I am concerned that due to this case, we are glorifying and immortalising a person who had in fact been convicted of other crimes. This was not a man who was an innocent bystander caught up in a bad situation. He had done wrong things too. I am not saying he hadn't paid for his sins and wasn't entitled to a fair go. There is absolutely no excuse for how he was treated. But what we don't have is all of the facts. We don't know exactly what took place before the scene which was captured on camera, and we don't know what the rest of the picture looks like. Would the same things have occurred if the victim was a white man? We simply don't have these answers.

But once again, this does not excuse bad behaviour and the fact that no human should be the victim of such treatment. There is definitely evidence to suggest that some behaviours are racially motivated. And this is not isolated to people of coloured skin; this is happening everywhere. But does this incident justify the bad behaviour which resulted in looting, destruction of property, the death of innocent people in almost every city of the world. In my opinion, that is not the way issues get resolved.

And what about the ripple effect which led to the removal of statues and other monuments? In my opinion, we do not have the right to destroy something that our ancestors erected. They must have had their reasons. Whether it is positive or negative, history is just that, history. It is something that has happened in the past under a set of circumstances that existed at that point in time. To judge history based on the standards we have today is wrong. We have come a long way in our evolution, and at times it feels we haven't. To destroy a statue based on a set of ideals which exist today, without taking the time to understand the context within which the decisions were made in the past, is immature and completely wrong. Leave history alone. We have a responsibility to learn from the past and evolve into the future. We too, are making history right now. We are not to know what standards will exist in the future and how our actions will be judged at that time. All we can do is make the most of what we have today and base our decisions on what is best under the current circumstances.

If each of us treated the next person with respect and compassion, the world would be a better place. 'What about the people I don't like?' I hear you say. If you don't like someone walk away and cut them out of your life completely. There is no point trying to hurt someone just because they wronged you. The best revenge is to walk away with your head held high and be successful or happier elsewhere. This may sound like a simplistic view, but it should not be too hard to be a good person. None of us are born bad, we become that way.

Let karma do its thing. Nothing gets past the Universe after all.

AN UNEXPECTED DETOUR

I must confess, I have always had a peculiar fascination with the end of the world and doomsday theories. I am not sure why, but it has always piqued my curiosity.

In what seems like it was only yesterday, I can recall the feeling as we approached the turn of the century, and the doomsday prediction dubbed the 'millennium bug' threatened to cause a major catastrophe. After spending much of the year ensuring systems had the appropriate patches applied, we waited with bated breath as the clock struck midnight on 31 December 1999. I recall we stayed home to celebrate that night ... *just in case.*

I am not sure what we were expecting to happen. Many believed the clock would become stuck forever at the stroke of midnight. That nothing would tick over because nobody had planned for the new set of numbers. It seemed so final, the number 99. Would ATMs work? How would we access our money in the bank? Would we be stuck forever in 1999? Against all odds, humanity triumphed once again.

There was similar talk about 2012, which signified the end of the Mayan calendar. Once again, there had been no foresight past that point. The 12th day of the 12th month of 2012 became a significant date for a set of very strange reasons. They even made a Hollywood blockbuster about it. But that day too came and went quite uneventfully, as it turned out.

Our current situation doesn't have the same 'doomsday appeal' but it is nevertheless a significant time in history, the likes of which most of us alive today would never have lived through before. And while it doesn't appear to be the end of the world, it does feel like it is the end of the world as we know it. The use of masks, hand sanitiser, perspex barriers and sticky markers on the ground, the recording of your movements, the taking of your temperature and the need for distance are creating a new set of social norms. Sneezing or coughing in public, even if undertaken carefully and mindfully, is almost frowned upon. Catching the flu could almost make you an outcast, through no fault of your own. Will isolation become a new habit? Are these new measures here to stay, to some extent?

I am seeing people banished and attacking each other on social media for having a different view from their own.

I am seeing people call out the behaviour of others while they practise the same hypocritical behaviour. We are becoming even more sensitive than we already were. And political correctness has gone to a whole new level. We are now even questioning the names of household brands that have been around forever. We need to get a grip and focus on what is important, because instead of becoming a more educated and tolerant society, we are actually going backwards at a hundred miles per hour.

Before we knew what the word 'covid' meant, I thought I was travelling down the road just fine. Staying in my lane, cruising along to my music of choice until … *screech—hit the brakes, a roadblock.*

Damn it! I had not anticipated that. In all of my calculations, I did not factor in a change in course. Well, not quite yet anyway. There was no getting around this one. The signs were clearly telling me that it was pointless to continue down this particular road. It was time to consider taking a detour.

Not quite sure of which way to go, I decided to pitch a tent in that spot for a while. To enjoy the peace and quiet, breathe a sigh of relief, shake the weight off my shoulders and just sit and contemplate. For, you see, not only is this a detour, this particular block in the road is potentially life-changing. Where I go next is a huge decision and it will inevitably shape the future. And I for one don't want to make a mistake this time.

Rewind just a little in your mind to imagine the point at which I was comfortably driving down a long stretch of safe road. Picture this: me, in a classic red vintage car. Roof off. Tapping the steering wheel to the beat of a Coldplay song, my hair secured under a floral scarf. My sunglasses shielding out the bright rays of a glorious day. You get the picture? There I was, cruising along, until, out of nowhere, it started to rain. No warning. No time to prepare. Unable to see through the haze. Scrambling to find the button to close the roof. Nowhere to escape the mess that was about to transpire. And to top it all off, a roadblock! The road ahead was no longer a viable option. It was definitely time to take a detour.

And I call it a detour because I know that there is a point in the road where I will be able to get back on it, although it is likely to look a little different to the one I had previously imagined. But that's the beauty of a vivid imagination, you can adjust it easily to reflect a different picture. When I find the right road again, I can continue travelling towards my purpose. I believe I was on the right road all along. The detour means it's just going to take a little longer and there are a few things I need to acquire along the way.

Sometimes you have to take a great big step backwards; right back behind everyone else on the starting line, in order to create enough intensity and determination, and to gather enough speed for the sprint to the finish line.

Some people I know are actually so pleased to have had covid-19 as an excuse to hide behind. But that's all it is, an excuse. A convenient time when change is occurring so rapidly that you can easily throw in a few more changes, because in someone's mind it is justified.

So what happened, you ask?

For those of you who have read my first book, you will recall that I have worked with my family since I was in my early twenties. I had taken a break from the business a few times, and after the latest time, I remained as a full-time contractor to the business. Well it seems that I am no longer relevant. That I no longer fit, in a business which is part owned by my own family, but in which the family have absolutely no relevance. And it was very easy to get rid of me because on paper I was a contractor after all and according to them, they owned me nothing.

Once again, with respect, I will not go too far into the detail. Mostly because I refuse to be seen as a victim or to give this issue any more oxygen than it deserves. It is more important to highlight the lessons learnt as a result. Boy, I am sick of this particular lesson. But I have now mastered it, and I am so relieved to be in a position where I can say that. The last time I walked away from the business it was due to a need to break a vicious cycle. The choice to do this caused me a great deal of disadvantage, while the real culprits remained perched in their position of security. Don't be a martyr, they said. But did I listen? No, I didn't!

So I bit off my nose to spite my face, didn't I? Even though I knew it would be more than my nose that would be bitten off in the long run. Yes, you guessed it ... in the end, it bit me in the backside!

I actually have to stop and have a chuckle to myself as I realise I must sound like a person who continues to attract the same drama into her life. If all of these things didn't happen to me, what would I even have to write about? Not again, I hear you say, And the Universe, well, she's just rolling her eyes yet again, saying, 'I told you so. You have to do it the hard way, don't you?'.

The moral of the story here is when faced with an obstacle, you get to choose how you will handle it. You can either play the victim and fret about how you have been hard done by, or you can use it as fuel to make yourself work harder, which is what I intend to do.

I refuse to be made to feel worthless by someone who is yet to prove their worth. My age has been referred to as if it was a major impediment. Talk about inappropriate. I have been told I am no longer relevant as I don't fit with someone's idea of a future direction. Am I going to let some idiot tell me who I am? Hell, no! The beauty of being *my age* is that I have had a lot of time to get to know exactly who I am. I don't need to be told!

I am shaking off the last of my old feathers and moving on. I am going to speed through the detour, carefully of course, until I am firmly back on the road where I belong. And heaven help anyone who tries to throw me off course again!

ALMOST FIFTY AND FEELING FABULOUS

I started writing my first solo book when I turned forty. I published it at forty-eight. As a result of this universal shutdown, I now find myself with more time to pursue my love of writing and am penning this book. And from where I sit right now, I am in full view of the next decade which awaits me, my fifties.

Unlike the feelings I had when I turned forty, which were both daunting and enlightening at the same time, I am feeling extremely at ease about turning fifty. In fact, I am very proud to be my age, and very comfortable in my own skin. As I prepare to close out this decade of my life, it is clear that it is the one which has challenged me the most, taught me the most, and prepared me for what I am absolutely sure will be the next best decade of my life.

I used to fear getting older, but now I am grateful for the maturity and the wisdom that comes with it. And there is no way I would ever go back, other than perhaps to tweak the story, just a little bit, here and there.

Reflecting on one's past, it is possible to assign a theme to every decade of life, give or take a little. Childhood lays the foundations. Before you are ten years old, your family unit is everything. You have nothing to worry about and everything is taken care of. But any trauma that occurs during this time can have a long-lasting impact. It tends to rear its ugly head much later in life.

Between ten and twenty years a huge shift occurs. This is a lengthy period of time for someone so young. A child to an adult; there's so much that has to happen to get you there. Friends become the centre of your life. Family are important, but they take a step back. They remain a means of support and are there to lean on whenever you need them. Puberty, and all that goes with it, will scare the living daylights out of you, as you struggle to come to terms with who you are and where you fit in. You do your best to navigate through. Friends come and go. There's a fair bit of experimentation with different things. You either choose to follow those around you, or you stand firm, cemented in your values. The highlight of the decade is usually the road to independence, getting your licence and finishing high school, because when you get to adulthood, well, you think you've made it. You've hit the jackpot.

Then, you enter your twenties and adulthood isn't all it was cracked up to be. You have to work, and you soon discover that the world is a competitive place. You suddenly find yourself at the bottom of the food chain once again. You realise that your parents were indeed right; your high school years were your best years, and you regret not having made the most of them. You have a newfound appreciation for your family, in particular your parents, who have been paying your bills. During this time, you may fall in love, and out of it, quite a number of times. But once again, there is a lot that happens in this decade. Who one goes in as at twenty is not the same person who comes out the other end at thirty.

It's different for everyone, but for me the thirties revolved around raising children. Having had my first child at 29, by 32 I was having my third. Done and dusted in no time. But that was the easy part. The years that followed were filled with breastfeeding, dirty nappies, loads and loads of washing, toilet training, preparing for kindergarten and school, and running around to sporting events. During this time, I relinquished who I was, to a certain extent, having taken a step back in my career and put all of my drive and ambition on hold. I was caught on the mummy train and committed to my purpose, which at that time, as well as surviving, was focused on raising my kids to be humble, grounded, resilient, curious and well-adjusted individuals. Whether I have succeeded in this endeavour is yet to be seen, but it's not looking too bad so far.

The forties, well, I have written a book about what that looked like for me. The reason I wrote that book was that I was seeing similar themes play out for the people around me of a similar age. Even today, I have friends who are in their very early forties and I am watching them begin to question things around them. In my opinion, the forties are a time of reflection and consolidation. Usually by then, one has the maturity and enough life experience to make some important evaluations. In other words, it is the time of 'wake-up calls' and, as I like to call it, 'the time when some of the lights are starting to switch on'.

It's a time when you start to shift the focus away from everyone around you and you start to make some internal evaluations. You look more closely at relationships, work, family and friends, and you come to the realisation that perhaps you don't need so many things in your life. You only need things that enhance it and add value. You start to get a niggling feeling that there is possibly more to life. You begin to consider the trajectory you are on and start to measure the likelihood of achieving those goals you had set out in your mind. Time to make some assessments. Are those goals realistic? Should you settle for less, or should you get on your bike and start peddling a little faster?

All around me I am seeing people starting to wake up. Starting to question their purpose in life and whether they are living their best life. I believe this is a natural occurrence during your forties, as you prepare for the years ahead. People, in particularly, women, are shedding the many layers of their conditioning and beginning to realise that the key to living a fulfilling life actually starts with and depends predominantly on themselves. Never has there been a time like today, where women are so independent and so willing to choose themselves, knowing that by doing so, they are indirectly benefiting those who rely and depend on them the most.

I used to think happiness was a goal to strive for. I thought it was something you arrived at one day after you had sifted through all of the things that stood in the way of you and your happiness. It's a difficult thing to define, happiness. It's intangible and very easily slips through your fingers. At one moment you think you have found it, and the next moment you wake to find it has been taken away, just like that. Like love, it appears that happiness is subjective and illusory, and somewhat conditional on so many other factors being in alignment. But that's not how this is supposed to work. Love and happiness are supposed to be unconditional, that is, they are consistent and independent of anything else which may be changing around them.

Love and happiness, whatever they mean to an individual, are not goals, but states of being. You spend your time in love and happy, at your core. It resides within you and is not subject to change, although it can sometimes be difficult to stay in that state of bliss. Things happen to try to shake you and test you. But you just know that it is there, underneath all of the piles of *stuff* that life will inevitably throw over the top of them.

I have spent much time trying to define what happiness means to me. I know full well that I am responsible for my own happiness, and conversely, I am not responsible for the happiness of others. That is their own responsibility. To me, happiness is a state in which I am grateful for all that I have. I am at peace with myself and the circumstances around me, even when they are negative. In fact, being in the state of (let's call it) grace allows me to confront the tests head on, with a clear and objective mind, and allows me to sift through the positive and the negative, taking the lessons and discarding the rest. I know that when I am residing in a state of grace, I am in alignment with my true self and will therefore attract, like a magnet, those things that are truly meant for my greatest good and, in turn, that of others.

Happiness, subjective as it may be, is something we all want more than anything in the world. Even if you think of it in terms of material objects, that is, you may think you want to own that sports car, what you are actually wanting is the *feeling* of owning the sports car. The happiness you feel because of it. Everyone defines happiness and success in different ways. Fortunately, there is enough of it in the world to go around. We all have the ability to be happy and successful just by believing we will be. Because we know how we want to feel, it is possible to attain that feeling every single day. The rest is all a bonus. Because don't forget, like always attracts like, and that is also true of happiness. The happier you are, the happier you are likely to become.

Go on, try it on, you will find that it really looks good on you!

I am excited about my fifties and let me tell you that I never thought I would say that. But unlike my forties, when I was still sifting through the garbage, right now it seems to have been sorted. I have cleaned up the mess and put things in their rightful place and I am ready to move on with much less clutter, only taking the things that I really need. While I can, I will make the most of my late forties knowing that the best days of my life are just around the corner, the years when I will do what I have always wanted to do. I will work hard on myself so I can be the person I have always dreamed of.

For me, happiness is the feeling I get when I am being true to who I really am—my most authentic self. When I am grateful for and mindful of the people and things I have around me. When I am surrounded by things that I love and things that create awe and wonder. When I have a goal and a clear vision of where I am going. When I am working on the things I am most passionate about. When I am making the next person feel better about themselves. When I am making a difference. When I am told that I have 'inspired' someone. All of these things light me up on the inside.

Coincidentally, it seems that as well as making me happy, these things are all connected to my purpose. But then again, there is no such thing as a coincidence.

PINA DI DONATO

A WORD WITH MY DAUGHTERS

When I was pregnant with my first child, I was indifferent about whether it would be a boy or a girl. I was blessed with a gorgeous little boy, who now at nineteen is not quite as adorable as he once was. Now he is extremely handsome.

My second child followed 23 months later. Again, I was indiffcrent, but secretly I wished for a little girl. And to my pleasant surprise, my wish was granted when my precious daughter Miss A was born.

Fast forward another nine months, quite unexpectedly, I found myself pregnant once again. With a pigeon pair already, I was, once again, indifferent to the baby's gender. For this reason, with each of my children, I didn't find out what I was having because I thought it would spoil the surprise. My baby was born in August 2004, a precious little girl, who will always be my baby, no matter how old she gets. Even now, at sixteen, she doesn't exactly like me referring to her as my baby.

When Miss K was born, I felt I was the luckiest person on earth. I had been blessed with three beautiful, healthy children, and specifically with two girls who would always share a special bond because they were sisters. And I get the special privilege to be in the background to watch this bond—which is not always a positive one—every single day.

It is difficult to raise children and becoming increasingly more difficult as time goes on. It was physically demanding for me when they were little, but I guess I was lucky to have them all go through the same stages together. Raising boys and girls is quite different, and as they get older, I find the demands are more of an emotional nature. Boys, I find, are not great at communicating their feelings, preferring to leave much of their feelings bottled up inside. Girls, on the other hand, have an innate need to express themselves, often seeking validation and reassurance, which can be draining and repetitive for a mother. And sometimes it reminds me that I too was once a teenage girl.

As their mother, it is my responsibility to lead by example and to model the values that I have tried to instil in them. My responsibility is the same when it comes to all three of my children, but with my daughters, I feel I have an additional layer of responsibility, not because I am their mother, but because I am a woman. It is in this capacity that the behaviour I model to them will have the greatest impact.

So, I thought I would take this opportunity to write an open letter to my daughters.

> To my beautiful girls
>
> Isn't it interesting how most people look twice when they see you together? Some just think it; others actually ask the question: 'Are you twins?' But even though you look similar, you are very, very different.
>
> Then people look at me to determine if either of you look like me. And the answer to that one is pretty obvious, whether you like it or not. It's true, one of you is my carbon copy, and it is fascinating for me to see my younger self in you. I get to see how others may have seen me when I was young, something I could never see for myself. What this also highlights to me is that I didn't really value myself as much as I should have.
>
> But while the physical similarities are obvious, it is the one who looks less like me on the outside who has grown to be more like me on the inside. Either way, you are both stuck with me; the good and the bad.
>
> However, I am less interested in the extent to which you remind others of me, and more about each of you being your own individual selves. It is a challenge having two girls

so close in age. There is a temptation to apply a 'one size fits all' approach, making it much easier on me. But that wouldn't be very fair on you, would it?

You each have the right to be yourselves and my role is to provide the space for you to do that. A space that is safe. A space where you belong and where you are seen and heard. I know you think that I am not always effective at doing this, but I am trying my very best.

The greatest gift I can give to each of you is for me to be the best person I can possibly be. In doing this, I can provide you with a living example. You are free to take my examples, not as something set in stone, but rather as something to learn from and adapt to suit yourself. I don't want you to be like me. I want you to be the best person you can possibly be, in the same way that I am trying to be. I have no doubt that will look very different to you.

As a mother, it is tempting for me to want you to be like me. And this is what I used to think. Now, I would say that I hope I am providing you with a good enough example and giving you meaningful advice so that you can make your own choices. I don't necessarily want you to be like me. In many cases, I would rather you be the opposite. Seeing it in this way is only possible once I remove the labels that define me as your mother and you as my daughters. It is only when I can look at each of you as unique individual human beings that I can view it from this angle.

Both of you have something unique to offer the world, and despite your physical similarities, you couldn't be more different in that respect. My wish for you is that you find that thing that makes you want to jump out of bed in the morning and be excited about the day that lays ahead. And I don't care how high you aim, as long as you have your head tilted upwards and you are looking at the sky. Don't look down, nor back over your shoulder. There are only two places you need to apply your focus. Upwards and forwards.

Don't ever settle for anything less than you deserve and don't ever let anyone tell you who you are or who you should be. Not even I get to do that as your mother, therefore nobody else should have that right either. Your mission in life, if you wish to accept it, is to discover who you are piece by piece, all on your own, through good times and hardships. I will always be by your side to guide you. When you call for me, I will run to meet you, but I will never get in your way.

I have tried my best to raise you both to be confident women and to have healthy self-esteem. This is extremely important as there are so many areas of life trying to tell us that we are not good enough. I have tried to lead by example in this respect, by valuing who I am and accepting myself for all that I am. You both know that I encourage you to be your natural, beautiful and authentic selves, and I am so proud of who you have grown to be. I have taught you that make-up and other embellishments are okay, as long as they are used sensibly to complement what you already have, not to cover you up and make you into something you are not.

The opposite of covering up is exposure, and this is a lesson we have talked about many times. I am not strict on what you wear but I do tell you when something is not appropriate. And I know that at times I have not been as tactful as I should have been, and perhaps caused you some embarrassment among your friends ... whoops, I am sorry for those times. But what I apologise for is how I delivered the message, not about the message itself. I have taught you that there is a fine line between classy and trashy, and that it is you who gets to decide which side of that line you want to be on. You are free to wear whatever you wish, but unfortunately it will create a perception. Now, I am not one to care too much about what others think, but I do worry about how you may come to regard yourself. As I said, the way you want to be regarded is totally up to you, but it is based on what you choose to show the world.

One day, I hope you find love. True love. But I also hope you don't. I hope you make some mistakes before you eventually get there. And I know the mistakes will challenge you and make you feel like your world is crumbling down around you, but it will also teach you how to define love and show you what you truly value in this regard. Don't ever be in a rush to settle for anything less than what your heart truly deserves. And if you make a mistake, I will be there to help you pick up the pieces and make yourself whole again.

Please don't allow your happiness to be dependent on any one thing or any one person. Make it part of who you are every day. I know this sounds unrealistic, but just try. Try to see the light in things. Try to see the positives. Even on the darkest days, there is always something to cling to and to give you hope. As long as the sun rises each morning, there is always a fresh new opportunity to right any wrongs or mend any mistakes.

I am so completely blessed to have three beautiful children, and in that, two gorgeous daughters, who I know will be my greatest companions through life. I am so proud of you both and I hold so much hope for your future. I hope I have been the mother you wished for, and when I haven't been, I hope you can forgive me. I don't want to be your best friend; I am your greatest fan, your first teacher and a mentor for life. But most importantly, you and I, we share an unbreakable bond. There are only three people in this entire world who know what my heart sounds like from the inside, and you are two of them!

Go forward with strength, courage, dignity and grace. I will be walking alongside you, every step of the way.

Your loving Mamma

Now, just because I have written a note to my daughters, it doesn't mean I treat my son any differently or less well. For him, my advice is essentially the same, but my responsibility is to enable him to grow into a good man. A man that is grounded and humble, and confident and well rounded, but one who also understands that a woman is his equal and should therefore be respected as such. Again, whether I have been successful remains to be seen, and I would say that raising a son in this respect has been much more difficult considering my underlying culture. And, as much as I hated the distinction when I was growing up with my own brothers, I find that some of that conditioning is so deeply ingrained in me that it happens unconsciously. But I have two daughters who constantly remind me that there is no place for such double standards in our household. It's still tough, nevertheless, and he still gets away with things he shouldn't. I do my best to remain mindful of this and try to take steps to undo what has been done, mainly as a result of my culture.

That brings up quite an interesting point, relating not only to gender, but to children more broadly. On one hand we say we should treat boys and girls equally, but on the other hand, we should treat them individually. And I agree that there should be no distinction as to what they can or can't do, based on their gender. But when you remove the gender label, they should be treated as individual humans as opposed to being treated equally just because they are all my children. Viewing them as individuals means that we can see their weaknesses and strengths in the same way as we can see these things in other human beings. Just because they are all my children, it does not make them all carbon copies of one another. They are all unique and have the right to be encouraged to be so.

When I was young, and very much because of my culture and the fact I was the only girl, what was expected of me at home was different from what was expected of my brothers. The boys were encouraged to look after the outdoors and to go to work. The women were the homemakers, the cooks and the cleaners and the representatives of the family when it came to visiting others or attending funerals. Different rules for different genders.

But I was not your 'typical female'. And come to think of it, neither was my mother, who stood alongside my father, doing all the tough jobs when they were building their business. I was very much focused on education and career, and being a homemaker was something I knew would come with the role of being a wife and mother. However, it was not what I aspired to be. And although my brothers and I worked together, we all had very different personalities, strengths and skills. But it seems that while it was okay to have different rules at home, work was another story. At work, it was insisted that we all were treated the same. As a result, we were all brought down to a common denominator. It didn't matter what any one of us did in terms of our contribution; we were all the same. I can't begin to tell you the repercussions these types of rules have, when others fail to see your worth as a unique individual regardless of your surname.

It takes a lot of effort to restrain yourself from applying the 'one size fits all' approach, and for me this is particularly true for my girls who are so close in age. But I would not be doing them the justice they deserve if I lumped them all into the same category. I would be failing to see their strengths and help them to play to them and their individual passions, and to note their weaknesses and to help them rise above them.

And with regard to my son, my wish is that he aspires to reach the heights that he is destined to reach. He has been blessed with many talents, and this was evident from when he was just a little boy. There is no limit to what he can achieve provided he wants to.

He also has a wonderful depth and an awareness that is way beyond his years. He has strong values and beliefs, and is an advocate for social justice, just like his mum. I am extremely proud to have such a fine man in my life. He used to look up to me, but now, given his height and stature, I find myself looking up to him, and not only in the physical sense.

Being a parent is one of life's most challenging roles. Despite all that has been written on the topic, there is only one way to learn to raise children, and that is to go through the process of raising them. The best way to do this is to be the ultimate role model, to set healthy boundaries, to enforce them consistently, to guide and mentor, and to give them enough space to make and learn from their own mistakes. And while you are at it, give yourself a break. You can only do the best you can with the tools you have. At times you will feel as though you have failed, but you will get up and try again. And you will love your children fiercely, even though you will not always like them. As much as they defy you, you will forgive them and they will forgive you, although not as easily as you will forgive them, I am afraid.

That's what parents do. They give love and support without imposing conditions.

THE PATH OF LEAST RESISTANCE

I can't believe I used to think that everything had to be difficult. That if things were not as challenging as I thought they should be, then they wouldn't lead anywhere. Boy, did I have things back to front. To me, the more stress I endured and the harder I worked, the closer I would supposedly be to my goals. It would mean I was on the right path. Life is not meant to be easy. Haven't you heard this said so many times?

But it seems that life is actually not meant to be as hard as I thought. It is the resistance and the blockages that make it difficult. But once you work through the challenges and learn from them, and evolve, then the road ahead will become much smoother.

I know what you are thinking. You are thinking that I am being irrational, that I am taking a far too simplistic view of the world. I understand what you're saying. I used to think in precisely the same way.

In order to understand it, I had to see it for myself.

Imagine for a moment that life is made up of many different paths which make up a huge and complex maze. The aim is to find your way to the finish line. You set off in hope that you will not come across too many obstacles and that the path to the other side will be uncomplicated and smooth. This particular maze has a series of challenges made up of dead ends, crossroads, illusions and doorways. The dead ends will mean there is no way forward. In this case, you either give in and accept where you are, or you backtrack a little to find another work around. The crossroads present a choice to be made based on what you know at that given point.

The doors, however, represent opportunity. The doors are either opened, closed or fully locked. Your job is to try to open the ones you encounter along the way and decide if you will take the opportunity presented.

For those who have read my first book, you may recall the dialogue about doors. They either open easily or they don't. When they open easily, take this as a sign that you are on the right path. When you encounter resistance, it may be an indication that this particular road is not the best option. You can insist if you like; it really is your choice. But if you take the less than optimal path you may encounter a range of obstacles along the way. That less than desirable path may still lead you to where you need to go, but it may take quite a bit of pain and a handful of lessons to get you there. When the path is clear, it is just meant to be. It is not hard work, because at that point, you have already dealt with all the crap and learnt the lessons to get you onto this smooth section of the path.

Let me give you a couple of examples.

As you may be aware, my first book took me many years to write, and although the intention wasn't always to publish it, it had in fact always been the dream. It is something I thought of often. I could feel how it felt, and visualise how it would look. Did I actually manifest it into reality? What do you think?

This is the way I see it: writing and communicating must be connected with my soul purpose. That would make sense. It is my greatest passion and I now know it is a skill I have been blessed with. Writing in a way that inspires others gives me joy and lights me up on the inside. So, if writing is part of my purpose, it must be true that it is so much a part of who I am that I just know it will happen. In fact, I will make it happen because I am in alignment with it happening, and it is for my greater good and that of those around me. All I need to do is bridge the gap from point A to point B, in order to reach the goal.

Like everything else, it is a process. In my mind, I imagined how difficult it would be. I was talking about becoming a published author after all; it's not that common among people I know. It had to be difficult, right? It just wouldn't do the process justice to be any other way.

But as it turns out, when something is just meant to be, the things that you need in order to get you there seem to just present themselves, often in the simplest of fashions. If you are aware, you will recognise these things I like to call 'cookie crumbs' and follow them to see where they lead. When you trust yourself enough to back yourself. When you are able to tune into what you know to be true in your gut, it can make it all look like an effortless journey. What it is, in fact, is all of the pieces you need falling into the right place at the right time. In the end, your soul purpose is something you signed up for before you were born. You are meant to get there in the end. You can make it either difficult or easy. It depends on whether you trust yourself enough to unravel and follow the clues and put yourself in alignment with the end goal.

Back to my example. Because I thought the journey of publishing a book was meant to be fraught with obstacles and danger, I had in fact built up a fear around it. Why would anyone publish my book? Who would want to read it? What if it doesn't sell? Is the writing good enough? How will I be judged out in the public arena? Can I handle the critics? Once it was out there, I knew I couldn't exactly take it all back, could I?

Fear is what prevents us from seeing the path for what it actually is. Fear creates an illusion that applies an overlay to the actual picture, complicating it with blockages and obstacles. The fear tells us that in order to travel along that particular path, the obstacles need to be eliminated. But what would happen if you realised that the fear itself was actually causing the blockage? That it was indeed possible to achieve the dream if you only worked on removing the fear? Would it remove that veil of illusion and show the path for what it really is? I believe it would.

I remember it clearly. I was in bed and I was scrolling through my phone, as you do on a Saturday morning, when one of the beautiful souls I know, who I hadn't been in contact with for a long while, sent me a message in response to one of my social media posts. Totally unrelated to book publishing. We had a brief chat about where we were each at in life, and she told me she was about to publish a book. 'Wow', I replied. I was so proud of her. I asked about the process and she said the first thing to do is to engage a professional editor. I am not great at asking for information, but on that particular day, I asked if she wouldn't mind sharing the contact details for her editor, who she spoke very highly of.

Now, I have been around the block a few times, and what I know to be true is that there are no such things as coincidences. It was absolutely no coincidence that I was having an early morning chat with someone I hadn't come across in years. I knew this was a message I had to take seriously. I wasted absolutely no time in messaging the contact she provided and introducing myself. Before I knew it, I had sent off my completed manuscript and she had agreed to take on the job. The editing process went smoothly and without too much work on my part. Part one had been successfully accomplished.

Part two. It was my lucky day, as the editor was connected with a boutique publishing company, and after editing my manuscript, I boldly asked whether she would consider publishing my book. Before I knew it, I was signing a publishing agreement. I had a preconceived fear of big publishing companies. I didn't want to be treated as a number. I didn't want to lose my voice and identity as an author. Serendipitously, I had in fact been placed on the same path as a publishing company that had been established for people just like me. Once again, an example of perfect alignment.

I honestly thought the Universe had placed all of these people and circumstances in my path. The whole process was just flowing so smoothly that I almost had to question whether there was something I was missing. Surely, it couldn't be this easy, could it?

Now, in all of this, I am not trying to simplify the process and make it look like I have had everything handed to me on a silver platter. I have had to put in the time and the hard work. But you see, the work is not that hard when you are doing something you love to do. It really doesn't feel like you are working. The word 'work' tends to have a mundane, negative and uphill battle kind of feel about it, doesn't it? It really doesn't have to be that way.

When you are operating at the level you need to be at in order to achieve your goals, the process just seems to flow. When you align with the people that are meant to help and guide you through that journey, this also helps the flow. When all of the elements required to help you to fulfil your purpose present themselves *just like that*, you need to trust that you are on the right path.

I have so many stories just like that one.

Another happened to me recently when I applied to do a senior executive Master of Business Administration (MBA). Again, it was another thing I had always dreamed of doing. It was connected with my dream of being a true and authentic business leader. People around me tried to tell me that I didn't need a piece of paper or a set of initials after my name to prove my worth. And while I appreciated the sentiment and the faith in my abilities, I knew in my soul that this was not true at the level at which I aspired to operate. My dream is to change the world in some capacity and to leave a footprint. I felt I wasn't quite there yet.

Working for my family for so many years restricted my opportunity to develop certain skills. I was cognisant of the fact that there was a considerable gap between where I was and where I needed to be. I also needed to plunge into a world which was well outside of my comfort zone, in order to grow and gain confidence. It is a drastic move at my age, but one that definitely excited me.

Was I scared? Am I scared? Shit, yes! Absolutely petrified! Am I going to let fear put a veil of illusion upon my path this time? No, I am not. I am totally prepared to face my fears and stare them down until I win. As I told the program director in my interview when asked, why this and why now? My reply: 'At almost fifty, I can settle for what I have achieved until now. I don't really have to study an MBA, but I choose to for me; not for a job or a potential outcome, but for me to fulfil my purpose. And make no mistake about it', I continued, 'I do in fact want to change the world'.

Once again, this process of being offered a place to complete my MBA was a smooth one, despite all the fears I had concocted in my mind. The application process, the interview and being told at the end of that interview that I was the type of candidate they were looking for thrilled me to bits, although it once again had me questioning whether or not I had missed a piece of this particular puzzle. It just seemed to flow so effortlessly.

But what I learnt is that when you are in alignment and focused on something you truly want, and that *thing* is in line with your purpose, then the road to getting there is not meant to be difficult. When you are on the path where there is no resistance, you are in fact on the right path.

I am supposed to write books and I am supposed to continue with my studies. If I wasn't, then I would have encountered resistance. And even though I am often tapped on the shoulder by one of my fears, I know that I can't let them stop me. I have come this far. It would be mindless of me not to continue to move forward.

Take it from me. I am a seasoned traveller of these sorts of paths, with lots of experience in mazes and merry-go-rounds.

Choosing to take the path of least resistance doesn't mean you are settling for a path which is the same as everyone else's. Every single human being has their own unique purpose and it is this particular path, once aligned, that does not present any resistance.

A person who is confident and self-aware may also choose to take the path less travelled, as opposed to the more common path which has been taken by many, the outcome of which is well known and a little more predictable. Taking the path less travelled is much less crowded and offers opportunities to leave a unique mark on the world. The uncertainty of this path and the risks you undertake highlight your courage, your faith and level of awareness. These are attributes to be celebrated and rewarded.

I hope you find the courage to venture onto that path, forging yourself a new path and leaving a trail everywhere you go.

CONNECTION MATTERS

Isn't it just so cool how you and I have connected? Right here and now, it's just you and me. You are reading what I have written, and I feel so privileged to have created this space where I can talk to you. You have given me your time and I couldn't be more grateful for that precious gift. So, thank you!

I have been talking a lot about me so far. How are you doing? I bet that wherever you are in the world, you have had an interesting 2020 as well. I hope that you have managed to extract some positives and some lightbulb moments from your experiences. We have all been forced to make a hell of a lot of changes. I hope your life hasn't been too adversely affected, and that when you look back at this time in history, it doesn't leave you with any significant scarring.

Whatever is going on for you right now, just remember that you are only human. You can't expect that every day is a good day. Even the most positive person in the world will be feeling conflicted and challenged in the face of today's world events. Be kind to yourself. Don't ask too much of yourself during this time. There must be a reason why we have been forced to take a step back from what we had come to view as 'normal' in our lives.

What is normal anyway? Is it normal to have a life which is a constant grind, where we zoom through the day ticking all of the boxes on our respective 'to do' lists? Or having to meet a whole range of expectations because that is just what we do. Where you have to be ready for anything that life throws at you, expected to catch and deal with that curve ball, quickly and effectively. And when your life feels like it is constantly under scrutiny and judgement, particularly when you fail to meet those expectations.

I am not sure whether what I used to do could actually be called living. I used to spend my days constantly out of breath, running from place to place, ruled by the clock and the threat of looming deadlines. There were never enough hours in the day and my life was a constant juggling act and a logistical nightmare. But still, I did it. Why? Because that's just the level at which I operated. Life is supposed to be hard, right? How can you appreciate the reward if you don't do the hard yards? You are meant to sacrifice, bleed, sweat or cry to make it happen. Turns out I was wrong.

I am not quite sure I could ever go back to that life, the 'old' way. I have just recently learnt how to breathe properly. I have slowed down so much that it is totally bizarre and out of character for me. Now, on days where there is a little bit of running around to do, it frustrates me to my core. Finally, I have learnt to work smarter rather than harder. I have also learnt that a lot of the things I have in my life are not necessary. I can still function without them. I don't like clutter at the best of time, so I intend to keep my life simple and clean. That is how I prefer to operate. In that way, everything is transparent and valued for what it brings.

Did it take a pandemic for me to figure all of this stuff out? That's a bit drastic of the Universe, isn't it? But it appears that I am not the only one who has had to learn that particular lesson. This one is on a grand scale. We are all guilty of similar offences.

So where to now? Like everything, this challenge presents us with positives and negatives, depending on our perspective. What it also presents us with is opportunity, and time to make things happen. For me it has given me the time to publish a book and write this one. This slowdown enables us to take stock, evaluate what is important in our lives, simplify, reset and go forward with a renewed sense of clarity. It is 2020 after all, and this is the time when things are becoming clearer. The time when we are encouraged to see things for what they really are rather than the small piece of the bigger picture that we are often only being shown.

I have no idea what our new 'normal' will be, but I do believe it will be different from what we have known it to be in the past. This is the time when allowances need to be made. It's time to understand those around us a little more. It's time to be more tolerant and less judgemental. This time calls for greater awareness and understanding of what our neighbour may be going through. It's also the time for those who are in a position to help to come forward to do so. It's time for kindness and compassion.

It's also a time to get creative. To find new ways of connecting and communicating. To find new ways to conduct business. We have all been thrown a huge, unprecedented curve ball and what we do with it could ensure we make it through these trying times. Connection is extremely important during this time. It can be very lonely when you can no longer enjoy the freedoms you used to take for granted. We are all missing the connections with our loved ones, our extended families and friends. This time certainly highlights the importance of those connections and makes us appreciate life in a totally different way.

As I write this chapter today, the state where I live is staring down the inevitable path of further restrictions. An unprecedented move to stage 4 restrictions would mean that we are unable to leave our postcodes. There may be a curfew imposed and the defence forces called in to enforce the restrictions. This really is starting to sound like a science fiction movie.

And as supermarket shelves are stripped bare for the second wave, we are having to repeat the lesson we didn't learn last time. Only it will be much more serious this time. I hope we finally get it, because we must all realise that this is adversely affecting us more seriously than the actual virus ever could. The consequences are actually frightening.

I often marvel at how strong and resilient humans can be. It's also true to say that I often marvel at how unconscious and lacking in common sense they can be. It's true what they say; it takes all types to make the world go round.

I used to be more judging of people. I believed you were either right or wrong. And of course, I liked to believe I was always right, so anyone who contradicted me would naturally be wrong. It took me a long time to accept that everyone was *right* based on their own perspective. Their view may differ from yours, but just like you, they believe their perspective to be right. Nobody in their right mind would enter into an argument knowing they were wrong. This would set them up for certain failure. And nobody actually strives to fail. We all strive to win.

So for me, it comes down to a matter of perspective. And one has to respect the fact that each of us is entitled to that perspective. You may not agree with what another person is presenting, but it is your choice whether you buy into it or not. Their view either aligns with yours or it doesn't. You can't force that issue. To do so would cause you great discomfort.

And it goes even deeper than that. It helps you to understand why someone has a particular perspective if you filter through the top layers of what they are presenting to expose the conditioning and the value set that sits underneath. Our values are based on what we have been taught and the structures surrounding that. Each of us has a different set of values, and it's important that we try to understand where someone else is coming from.

Looking at situations and people objectively in this way removes any sort of judgement. Don't forget that there may be someone on the opposite side to you who doesn't actually agree with your perspective either, and the best thing they can do for you is to not judge you.

Once you accept that in life you cannot be all things to all people, you release a heavy burden from your shoulders. If you be the best person you can possibly be, primarily to yourself, with no judgement of yourself either, you will be much more at ease. Not everyone in your life will like you. You cannot control whether others do or don't. But when you are authentically you, you will find that you will naturally connect with those who are very much like you, on the same level and the same frequency.

With everything that is currently happening in the world, I feel there is a lot of judgement. We are being tested in the most significant way, but I am afraid we are failing big time. Instead of progressing and working together, reserving our judgement of others and our opinions, we seem to be doing the opposite. This is not only counterintuitive. It is counterproductive.

So let me have my say for just a few minutes. In no way am I saying I am right. I am just presenting a view from my perspective.

There are a few very distinct groups of thoughts out there today. As is the case in any group, there are the leaders, the followers, the rebels and so on.

The first group, who I shall call the leaders, are mostly self-assured and objective when it comes to disseminating the facts presented to them. Like most others, this group are doing their best to protect themselves and those around them. They respect the rules and are mindful of the wider consequences of non-compliance, such as the effects on the economy and on the mental wellbeing of the community. They observe what the experts are saying but they also look beyond the information and ask the challenging questions. They also see the bigger picture in terms of how humanity can collectively work through the issues and make long-lasting and positive change. They don't buy into fearmongering, nor do they follow the crowds. They are usually the ones that stand back, take note, and wait before offering their perspective.

Then there are the followers. This group take this pandemic very seriously and not for all of the right reasons. Some of these people live in genuine fear for their lives and therefore do the right thing at all times and do not condone inappropriate behaviour from others, which is a good thing. They also do not hesitate to call out the inappropriate behaviour. They buy into what the media is portraying and are consumed by these events. This is not such a good thing. They spread fear, which is the true contagion, to those around them and are unable to objectively look at the facts and make up their own minds. They prefer to be controlled by others. They download apps and will be the first to line up for vaccines because that's what they have been told to do, without considering the why. This is what is expected of us. Compliance, obedience, follow the leader … but at what cost?

Then there are the rebels. They naturally go against what others are doing or what is being asked or expected of them. It is in their nature to fight for a cause, usually any cause which will draw attention to them. Take a look at those in Melbourne right now, 'the anti-maskers', who are out rightly refusing to wear masks, saying that being asked to wear a mask is a violation of their human rights. They defy the law and the enforcers of those laws, and in order to spread propaganda, they film their antics and upload them to social media.

Those in this group have very loud voices. They are disruptors, and yes, within this group, there are also leaders and followers. They have all sorts of theories based on conspiracies and other agendas. This group tends to make a bad situation much worse and the media absolutely love them as they are masters at providing newsworthy content. The media coverage of rebellious acts, such as were seen during the recent #blacklivesmatter protests, makes it appear that the groups engaged in this sort of behaviour are bigger and more powerful than they actually are. Fuelled by more fear and sensationalism, this other form of virus continues to run rampant within the community.

And then there are the right wing and the left wing of politics. These wings represent different political ideologies. The fundamental difference between the two revolves around the rights of individuals versus the power of government. The extreme left believe society is best served with an expanded role for government and centres around socialist views. On the opposite side of the spectrum sit the conservative right wing. They oppose radical change and wish to preserve traditional society and institutions. Their views are much more capitalist in nature.

To give you an example, in Australia we are mainly governed by two political parties, and some minor parties. The Australian Labor Party (ALP) have more socialist policies with a significant role for trade unions. They sit to the centre left. The Greens party sit to the left of the ALP. The Greens favour environmentalism, such as expansion of recycling efforts, the preservation of habitats, and deforestation. The Liberal National Party sit to the centre right. Their views are more conservative, and their focus is on preserving the institutions of our democratic society.

These political terms were born in France in the 18th century during the French Revolution. They are based on the seating arrangements in the French National Assembly. Those to the left supported the revolution and a secular republic as opposed to those on the right who supported the old regime and wanted to preserve a more traditional society.

It is becoming more and more apparent that the voices of the more extreme sides of politics are getting louder. It seems that we are now expected to adopt one of the sides over the other. The truth is, however, that most of us are finding it increasingly difficult to find somewhere to sit within the spectrum of politics. Although I may be somewhat conservative in my views when it comes to some traditional aspects, lately I find myself challenging these structures more and more. And while I support entrepreneurship and have an understanding of the capital world, I tend to lean a little more to the left when it comes to social and environmental issues.

So my question is: why do I have to sit anywhere in particular? Why can't I just walk around the outside, observing, taking in, making up my own mind? Some days I may align more to the left, other days to the right. In some cases, I might even take the extreme option. I want to move around, learn and change, rather than sitting still entrenched in a particular ideology. I want to be free to have different views, or to change them when I come across a perspective that makes sense to me. Isn't it my choice? Aren't I entitled to my own opinion? Don't I have the freedom to voice that opinion without fear of reprisal?

I used to think that was the case. I am not sure what is happening to society at the moment, but we are allowing fear to dictate our beliefs. Under the cloud of this fear, there is so much hate, judgement and unrest bumbling beneath the surface and often even in full view of the world. Why are we starting to turn against each other when the solution lies on the opposite end of that particular spectrum? The solution lies in working together.

I am beginning to see the fear manifesting in my children. They have a particular view which I encourage them to put forward at home. I would hope they have the courage to express those views outside our home too. But the fact is that they are feeling intimidated and bullied into having a particular view. And that view is expected to be according to that of the masses. A different view could potentially make you an outcast. That's right; the people who are protesting about discrimination are the ones discriminating against others. What they don't realise is that their words may be saying one thing but their actions are actually saying something much more powerful. As a mother, I encourage my children to form their own opinions based on what they feel about the facts and the arguments being presented. Now society is even trying to undermine what I am trying to instil in my kids: good values, kindness, compassion and confidence. I feel as if the world is currently working against me.

What the world is relying on is the fact that we are all followers to some extent. You only have to look at what we do on social media to know this is true. We press buttons which allow us to 'follow' what others are doing, and to gain an insight into their lives. There's nothing wrong with being curious and gaining ideas or inspiration, but many obsess about it and are totally consumed by it. We then base our choices on what we see others doing or buying, because if it is good enough for them, the decision is an easy one, right? If they appear to be successful, beautiful or happy then they must have the right formula. Why invent it for yourself when you can just piggyback off theirs? Hence when you look around our society, instead of seeing originality and confidence, you see a cut-and-paste version of those who, in social media marketing terms, are referred to as 'influencers'. That is their job title, and they get paid a great deal of money to influence all of those who follow them. The more followers they have, the more valuable they are to marketers.

We are told these platforms are a form of staying socially connected to our friends, and while all of that is a nice thing, particularly when you have loved ones spread across the world, the truth is that they capture a lot of our time and attention. It makes complete sense that social media advertising has become so big, and has completely blown traditional marketing, such as television, radio and print, out of the water.

The people behind these social media platforms are among the richest and most powerful people in the world. They have access to information about us that would blow your mind. And we feed it to them willingly. What we see on our feeds and what is dished up to us is determined by a set of algorithms designed to achieve certain outcomes. While social media appears to be free to us, the user, it makes a hell of a lot of money from advertising. It is generally very cost-effective and can be extremely targeted. What are they selling exactly? Social media platforms are all competing for your time and attention, and in turn, selling it to the highest bidder. And they go to great lengths to get it without you even realising. There is nothing natural or random about it, and it is time to understand that there is a great deal of manipulation behind social media, all for the purposes of making money, gaining power and control, as well as the ability to influence and infiltrate. We can't escape it, but it is in our best interests, and in particular, in the best interest of our children, that we are aware, and we learn to manage it. Social media creates an illusion for what is really happening behind the scenes.

Come on, you must have noticed by now how your social media feeds get flooded, not only by the things you may have googled, but by the things you *spoke* about with your friends, in earshot of your phone, even if it was in your handbag. Siri is eavesdropping into all of your conversations and then delivering the message to the marketers, who then in turn serve it up and feed you with it. It's as automatic, as instantaneous, and as frightening as all of that. Marketers rely on the fact that we are all followers. We all do it. We all use it. It has become so normal that we no longer even have to think about it. It is all done for us. And that puts us in a very dangerous position. When we allow robots and automation to make decisions, which they are programmed to make, rather than using our human gifts to make decisions and influence the way things get done, we are not acting in the best interest of mankind. We are merely playing into the hands of others.

I am constantly having to remind my children what is real, and what is manufactured in order to elicit a particular response from them. It takes a conscious and consistent effort to keep them focused on the bigger picture.

Once again it is all about perspective. Ask yourself the question. What am I being persuaded to see or do and most importantly why, and does all of that sit right with who you are and what you know to be true in your gut? That's the only place you will ever find the truth.

Learning to distinguish between your gut and your ego, well, that's another chapter entirely.

(MOTHER) NATURE IS CALLING

'Nature' conjures up images of lush green trees, vast blue oceans, rolling hills and serene waterfalls. The word itself is grounding, nourishing and replenishing. True to its name, there is nothing more natural and authentic than nature. It is not man-made or manipulated. It doesn't ask or wait for permission. It just does what it was designed to do. Just be itself.

Speaking of design. How intricate is nature? How very complex! Consider how all of the different elements of nature: all of the ecosystems, the trees, the plants, the birds, the insects, the sun, the rain, the stars, the planets, the sea, the tides, the sea creatures and all of the other animals, how they work together so effectively without words or instructions, no clear leader or rules to follow, other than the rules of nature themselves.

How is it that all of these elements just know instinctively what to do? They work together in perfect harmony, each element relying on the perfect alignment of all of the other elements in order to thrive. They work collaboratively because they know that their mere existence relies on the ability of every other element to fulfil its unique purpose. They all work together to achieve this end, not for their individual wellbeing, but for the collective.

Nature just continues to go through its cycles of birth, growth, death and renewal. No overthinking, just doing, being and accepting this as its mission.

There is no competition in nature and therefore every part wins. And every part benefits equally. No human on earth, no matter how smart they think they are, can replicate the masterpiece that is nature. This perfectly and intricately woven tapestry is precious and priceless. Who are we to question its worth or deny its beauty? How can we even think that it is possible to improve or alter it?

Nature is already perfect just the way it is. Now, don't you think we should all try to take a leaf out of nature's book?

And yet, instead of accepting it for what it is, we exploit it. We set about destroying its balance in our quest for power and material gain. We strip, pollute, destroy and eradicate because we believe that in our industrialised world we have a right to do so. We believe we are doing other humans a favour. How long did we think we could continue to do this before Mother Nature would ultimately hold us to account?

And here it is. A virus, which, as I have said, has forced us to be locked away to rest and reflect. It has closed down businesses. It has taken cars off the road and boats out of the sea. What an ingenious way to make a point, not just in one place, but in every single corner of the planet.

The time has come for a hard reset.

Mother Nature reminds us that she will have the final say. We may think she needs us. She doesn't. She can exist without us. We, on the other hand, cannot exist without her. From where I sit, this gives her the upper hand, don't you agree?

Recently, I came across a beautiful video clip, in Italian, doing the rounds on social media during the first wave of covid-19. A similarly themed video, voiced by actress Julia Roberts, also caught my attention. Although the two messages are similar, the latter reminds us, quite matter-of-factly, that nature will continue to exist, with or without us. Nature doesn't need people.

> How you choose to live each day, whether you regard me, or disregard me, doesn't really matter to me. One way or

the other, your actions will determine your fate, not mine. I am Nature. I will go on. I am prepared to evolve. Are you?

Nature is Speaking.⁹

And considering everything we have been through so far in 2020, it doesn't take much more convincing than that, does it? Her power is very apparent in my eyes.

I think Mother Nature is sending us a timely warning, and what we are being given is a unique opportunity to take a different approach. What we choose to do with it will determine the rewards we can expect to be receiving from nature in the future.

I tend to talk about nature quite a bit. I do this because I think it provides a great, living example which covers a great number of different topics. In practical and very selfish terms, it also provides me with the energy I need to overcome some of the challenges I face. To spend time in nature is grounding and connects me with the source of all things. There is nothing fake or calculated or deceiving in nature. It is all in perfect synergy, alignment and harmony. Perhaps this is why, in quite the opposite way to people, it provides peace.

I love the outdoors, even though I am not an adventurer in the physical sense of the word. I don't swim or climb mountains or hike in any serious way, but I do have a vast appreciation for all things natural and am rewarded by the energy I get by being outdoors.

My favourite place to be is by the sea. Call it the Pisces in me, but I find being close to the water incredibly soothing. The sea shows us many different aspects of itself, so no two days are ever quite the same. On some days, the sea is calm, with gentle ripples and crystal-clear waters. Other times it appears dark and angry and sitting quite high, its waves crashing to the shore. A constant movement forward and backwards. Looking quite unsettled and far from being at peace. But beautiful, nonetheless.

I like water. It can be a bit like me. Gentle and calm, pleasant and welcoming, or alternatively strong, fierce and bold when that is the order of the day.

The sea is extremely powerful. It commands respect. It can turn on you in the blink of an eye and it can unleash on you the worst form of punishment. That is true not only of the sea, but of nature itself. Consider the bushfires in Australia in the early part of 2020. And why shouldn't it be that way? Why should nature continue to put up with bad behaviour and those who seek to take advantage of it?

It's currently winter where I live. It can be cold and gloomy, adding a further veil of obscurity to our already interesting circumstances. But like many other stages in life, winter is one that many of us don't like, but one that we inevitably have to pass through in order to get to the warmer weather. Despite the cold, the sunshine is still evident from time to time. It is amazing how a little sunshine can make a world of difference to an otherwise melancholy outlook. I crave to feel the sun. It is the light that brightens up the day. It warms you up like a big giant hug, penetrating right through to your core.

And don't you think it's amazing how the sun just comes up in the morning, like, every single morning, without fail? Even though we can't always see it or feel it, we know it is always there. It's one of the things we know we can rely on, for sure.

The dawn of each new day brings about an opportunity to start again, to start fresh. The sun continues to shine regardless of what may have got in its way yesterday. Despite the clouds attempting to overshadow it and obscure it from view, it stands firm. Unaffected by rain, wind or any other force of nature. Confident in its power, it waits for the storms to pass, before continuing to fulfil its purpose.

The sun never doubts its purpose, nor is it distracted by anything threatening to overshadow it. It has faith that the unfavourable elements will eventually pass. Nothing gets in the way of the sun, no matter how hard it tries. Its job is to warm and illuminate the world. And it succeeds to that end every single day. The sun also knows when it is time to rest and renew, respecting its bedtime and conserving the energy it needs to do it all again tomorrow.

After all, the world is counting on it!

Even on the cloudiest days there is always an opportunity to find a silver lining. At this time of reset, we have been given a window of opportunity. The circumstances surrounding covid-19 have us trying things we have never done before. There is an increased sense of urgency around finding solutions quickly. Some are innovating as a means of surviving. Others are identifying gaps or specific needs in our economies and moving quickly to capitalise on them.

We have a couple of choices. Once this is over, we can go back to how things used to be. Or we can take this opportunity to mould our future a little differently. There is no doubt that things have to change. This is the time to factor in things that can help us make our world a better place and protect us against future threats, which we all know are looming near, even though many of us don't want to face that fact.

I have said it many times in this book. The only way forward is to work collectively towards a common goal.

That is the only way to ensure our ultimate survival. If we continue to work against one another, what awaits us in the future will surely make what we are facing today look like a walk in the park. How much more of your freedom do you want to have taken away from you?

It makes sense that the industries that will thrive in the future are 'green industries'. These include industries converting energy from fossil fuel to renewable energy, such as replacing gas and electricity with solar energy, moving to electric-powered vehicles and making buildings more sustainable through engineering solutions that take into account design and the use of appropriate materials.

Manufacturing industries have an opportunity to consider sustainable alternatives to all aspects of their processes. By slowly converting current practices to greener ones, businesses can slowly absorb the costs associated with becoming more sustainable. Costs will be offset by the fact that the businesses will be leaders and pioneers in their respective fields, and will be ahead of the curve when green practices are no longer an option but a means of survival.

This is where our focus needs to be if we are going to build a sustainable future. Our leaders are currently scrambling for ways to rebuild our economy and our livelihoods, and much of that is going to take a great deal of foresight, imagination and risk. If we rush this process and focus on short-term recovery, we are merely applying a bandaid solution, one which will inevitable come unstuck sometime in the future. We now have a unique opportunity to work out what we can do differently rather than just trying to reinstall the same program which caused us all of the trouble in the first instance. We don't need the same economy as before; we need a stronger and more resilient one. We need a more sustainable economy. And to achieve this, we have to get more creative and we need to stretch ourselves further than we have ever done before.

Our recovery should not be based on a moment in time, but rather on a platform from which we can work towards a system guided by jobs and inclusivity, a greater resilience and equity, and a focus on health and wellbeing for the planet and for all of the people on the planet.

How do we do that?

It will take a substantial change in the way we think, the development of higher standards for businesses to reach, and much more transparency and accountability. It will also take much sacrifice, from all parts of the equation. It is a trade-off, a compromise in the short term in order to invest in the long term. The time has come for all of us to 'invest in the long game'—that is, if we want to be around in the future.

What we currently have is a model where leaders are focused on short-term profits. While they are well aware of the long-term implications of this type of thinking, they continuously talk about the problems they face, and the challenges these bring, rather than focusing on the solutions that are required to sustain business in the long term. Perhaps they are not interested in the long term, as they are likely to jump ship before that.

Tomorrow's consumer looks very different from what we have become accustomed to. Even if we try to avoid it, there is absolutely no doubt that we will be held to account by future generations. It is no longer enough just to meet expectations when it comes to price and quality. The buyer of tomorrow wants to know what you are doing in terms of the environment, the community and your own people. There will be many more boxes that will require ticking in the future. Much more than the item they are buying, the consumer of tomorrow buys into a vision, a story. They want to be a part of the change. They want to buy into something much bigger than themselves. Businesses must understand and appreciate this fact if they are to remain relevant in the future.

It takes courage to turn your back on a model of business that has been used for years. It's easier and more cost-effective to follow others than to reinvent the wheel. Why reinvent the wheel? Because the time has come to do so. Just because something has worked in the past, doesn't mean that it can't be changed or modified to serve the future. One of the first rules of business is to serve the customer. But still, we are not really listening to what the consumer is expecting from us.

The events happening around us today highlight the questions we need to be asking. Take a good look around and tell me what you see. We are being given the clues as to what needs fixing. We need to focus on equal opportunity, to embrace diversity, and to be more tolerant. No more excuses as to why it cannot be done. We didn't think we could bring the world to a standstill either, but look at what we have been forced to do. Instead of serving their own interests, leaders need to focus on what is good for everyone, because doing so will naturally make people happier, more fulfilled and in turn, more productive. Everyone can win. We just have to work out how we make it happen.

Like everything else, it will be a process. And it will take courage. But we have to start somewhere. Someone has to make the first move. I am prepared to do my part. Are you?

TRUST YOUR GUT

Most of our questions already have answers, and the answers are already stored within us. 'How is that possible?' I hear you ask. Your gut, your soul, your intuition—call it whatever makes you feel comfortable—already knows the answers. The challenge is to learn how to tune into this part of you in order to extract the answers and bring them into your consciousness.

Your *knowing* knows the truth of all matters. It is discerning. It has the capability to read energy and circumstances extremely well. It will never lie to you. On the other hand, there is your *ego*. And although the word in itself sounds negative and egotistical, it really isn't. Your ego is your mind. It is where information is stored. It is where your thoughts are created. But just because you have particular thoughts, they are only thoughts; they are not necessarily the truth.

The ego is dangerous because if you don't learn to distinguish between what is just a thought and where that thought originated, those thoughts can shape your reality. All good, if they are productive and positive, but what happens when they are not?

There is a constant power struggle going on, between the gut and the ego, for those who allow it to happen. The ego always wants to win, so it tries to convince you that it is always right, going to great lengths at times to sway you. The gut on the other hand wants you to just trust it. Just trust what it is trying to tell you because it just knows, and it truly has your best interest at heart. It's positioned at your very core for a reason!

The ego is threatened by the gut and therefore tries everything in its power to overshadow it. It is the dark to the soul's light. Its power comes out of making you fearful. It uses fear to manipulate you. By telling you that you are not good enough or not worthy of things, it seeks to strengthen your dependence on it. It can be the source of a great amount of stress.

There is no question that the gut, or the soul, is always the right one to follow. It takes faith and trust, and that is not always an easy thing. By trusting your knowing, you bring yourself into a natural state of peace and awareness, because you just 'know'. You don't buy into the ego's attempt to sabotage this state of being. Once the ego sees that it can't win against your steadfast resolve, it tends to go back into its box. It rears its ugly head from time to time, just to make sure you haven't changed your mind; it's a sneaky little sucker. The aim is to get to a place where you can objectively consider what your ego is presenting to you and say, 'That's all well and good, thanks for popping by to point that out, but I have already dealt with that particular challenge and learnt that lesson. Now rack off!'

Fear is more marketable than its counterpart, and humans for some reason are hardwired to buy into fear. With all channels, social and otherwise, flooded with things that create more fear and a sense of lack, it is difficult to believe that anything else exists.

What we must understand is that those in power know that people do in fact respond to fear. They are also aware of what those responses will look like and they play on them. And until we realise that we have power to effect change, we will continue to be controlled and manipulated.

Consider this. We live in a world that, in terms of wealth and power, can be depicted as a pyramid. There are a great number of people at the lower levels of the pyramid and as you move up to the tip of the pyramid there are fewer. Power and wealth are mainly concentrated at the top, in relatively few individuals. The world appears to be controlled by a small number of people, or is it? We perceive that power is held at the very top. Why is that, when the power actually resides with the collective? Is it possible that we have the maths all wrong? Doesn't it make sense that the true power is where there are more people, and if all of those people developed one collective voice, then the people at the top would be forced to listen, wouldn't they?

So, in my opinion, it's all about the maths and the calculations. Note that I didn't say it was all about the numbers. Well, it is in the strength of numbers, but sometimes the numbers we are shown do not tell an accurate story.

Take the profits of a company, for example. Businesses have a very narrow and short-term view when it comes to outcomes. They tend to live by quarterly results and what the impact of these will be on their shareholders. Business leaders can often be a selfish lot. Positive short-term results look good for them personally, but how many of them are actually invested in the organisation for the long term, and more importantly, how many of them actually care about the company's people?

The results can be made to look really good on paper. Some creative accounting and some selective storytelling can often do the trick. Most often if the numbers stack up, no further questions are asked. Everyone gets a pat on the back and the relevant people get a bonus for a job well done. But who actually did the job, and where is their bonus?

Does anyone ever stop to ask how we arrived at those impressive numbers?' What I would ask is: 'Did we sacrifice anything to obtain the numbers? Have we forgone anything that is important? Have we cut any corners, sacrificed our quality, compromised our brand or reputation? How are our people doing? Are they engaged? Do they feel they are part of the team?'

In my opinion, it is not enough these days to take the numbers on face value. It's not enough to measure wealth without looking at it in the context of wellbeing. If you obtain wealth by sacrificing things that are important to the collective, then you are not doing anyone any favours. The metrics are not telling the full story.

I'll give you an example to demonstrate my point. In our economy, we measure unemployment. A lower level of unemployment indicates the economy is healthy and tracking in the right direction. While this is certainly true, how many of the people who are employed are happily employed, connected and fulfilled in their employment? How many of them are in the right job, and if not, why not? How do these jobs pay? How are the jobs distributed among diverse groups of people? What are the barriers which exist for diverse groups of people? Looking at the level of employment as a quantitative measure is very different from measuring it in qualitative terms.

I recently listened to a TED talk by the first minister of Scotland, Nicola Sturgeon. At the time of writing, Scotland is one of three countries measuring wellbeing as an economic indicator. The other two are Iceland and New Zealand. She went on to mention how, interestingly, each of these countries is led by a woman. Now, that is thought-provoking!

These countries are looking beyond the numbers and are shining the spotlight on the wellbeing of their constituents. This is a smart, brave and dynamic move by these inspiring women, who I have no doubt will prove to the world that things can be done differently, and it is about time!

When are we going to take our power back and effect real change? Let's face it, we are all sick of the usual political stories, strategies and games—and by using the word 'politics', I am not only referring to our governments. We are all sick of the negativity and the fear incited by the media. We are all sick of advertising which gives us the solution to the problem we never knew we had until they created it or brought it to our attention.

Back to my point about our failure to challenge the numbers. One very important consideration of any business decision must be: what is the impact of our decision on the environment? What strategies can we employ to reduce any negative impact which may result from our practices?

By my own admission, I don't always do what's best for the environment. I am not a careful and diligent recycler. I hear what people are saying about climate change, but it wasn't until recently that I actually started listening properly. It awakened me to the fact that I need to do my part.

So, you know all of those American doomsday movies, well that stuff is about to become real. If it's not in my lifetime, it will definitely be in my kid's lifetime.

'Houston, we have a problem …' and let me tell you, Will Smith, Brad Pitt, Matt Damon and Tom Hanks are getting a little too old to go save the world, so we are just going to have to do it ourselves.

What do we need to do? We need to get serious about this stuff. We ruined the planet by exploiting resources in order to give us more, make things cheaper, make life more convenient. We have become a greedy bunch who want what we want, and we want it now. Not happy to wait until watermelon is in season, we want it available all year round.

Seriously, what did we think was going to happen? We cut down trees and don't replace them. How do we think we are going to breathe when there are none left? We disturb the natural order of things by messing with ecosystems. We take what we want but we don't give anything back to replenish these natural resources. Like everything and anything, the planet needs to be in balance in order for things to work the way they should.

We humans have a lot to answer for, and while the discussion around climate change is getting louder, it's going to take an enormous amount of power to steer this ship so as to avoid a huge collision with an iceberg.

We can do it, but it needs to happen fast, and it needs everyone to be working together.

Remember when I said the power is in the collective. As consumers, we need to demand that governments do what is best for the planet, not what is best for businesses, not what's going to get them votes. We also need to hold businesses more accountable for the choices they make. We need to refuse to purchase certain things that are made without adequate consideration for the environment. We have to be serious, though; we need to accept that we can't have everything we want, when we want it, and at bargain basement prices. This is what caused the problem in the first place.

The power is in the people. We are the ones who vote in our governments; they work for us, not the other way around.

Consumers have the power. We are the ones purchasing the goods and services. Businesses exist only because of us. We demand what gets produced, we need to start demanding how it gets produced.

Shareholders are the owners of big business. They are the ones who hold our businesses to account. The executives work for them; they pay their wages. We have the power to tell them how we want things done.

Factory workers are the ones who get the job done. There are more at this level than at the top. We have the power to collectively effect change in our workplaces.

Why is it that we fear those who occupy the pinnacle of the pyramid? Why do we give them the power to dictate how things get done? They wouldn't be at the top if it wasn't for everyone else at the base, holding things together. This is where the true power lies, it's in the foundations, at the very core and in this case, it is very much in the numbers.

The quicker we realise that we have the power in our own hands and start speaking with one collective voice, the quicker we improve our prospects, both in the short term and in the long term, for our kids and those that come after them.

REAL VERSUS MANUFACTURED

As I said earlier, it's getting much harder to sort through the garbage. To determine what really needs to go for good, and what still has value and can be recycled for the better. It's becoming increasingly more difficult to distinguish fact from fiction, truth from propaganda, and real from manufactured.

In my opinion, the media have a lot to answer for. The six o'clock news has become an absolute joke. Once upon a time we could count on a fair and accurate recount of the day's headlines and main events. Now, we have to sift through what we are being shown in search of the hidden agendas, political alliances, not to mention the sensationalism, in order to reveal the truth. We are the ones having to make assessments about what is real and what is made to look real but doesn't quite reveal the full picture. Why can't they just read the news in a neutral and unbiased way? All we want is commentary on the facts—all of the facts. The news has become much like a soap opera or a tabloid magazine, those very cheap ones that use the headlines to hook you in.

And why does it have to be so repetitive? Do they think we are so incompetent that we actually need to have everything on repeat? Once again, this particular time in history is unveiling the weaknesses of these institutions. People are starting to ask more probing questions. The pandemic we are facing is very serious, and in no way am I trying to diminish the importance of that, but what we are not being given is full disclosure of the situation and context around the information. We are being drip-fed the information through a tube laced with fear and expected to swallow it.

Let me give you an example of the level to which the media will swoop to get a story or make the headlines themselves. They will tell you that it's in the public's best interest to know these things, but I would question exactly whose interest it is really in. Here is something that caught my attention in the midst of the current pandemic. While interviewing the premier of New South Wales, a popular television presenter said: 'If you want change to be effective, shouldn't you call it out when it's happening?'

I totally agree! And that's why I am calling it out. I think the media needs to pull its head in and report on things that are in the interest of the public, instead of pushing their own agendas. It was supposed to be an interview about the premier's handling of the covid-19 crisis. One would assume the premier was prepared for this line of questioning. It would also make sense to assume the premier would be expecting some tough questions, in particular with reference to her state's handling of the *Ruby Princess*, a ship which docked in Sydney. The passengers, some of whom were infected with the covid-19 virus, were allowed to disembark without being quarantined. But what she may not have been anticipating were the questions around gender issues within parliament.

In my opinion, this was a cheap shot. It really irritates me that the media can hide behind the guise of their so called 'freedoms'. To me, they are the ones who create much of the problem, as they dramatise and catastrophise everything, not because it is in the best interest of the public, but because it is in the best interest of their shareholders. Commercial television is called that for a reason. It relies on money from advertisers. Advertisers want to put their money into the shows that pull the biggest audiences. And what better way to capture an audience than through controversy and shock factor?

You only have to look at how reporters are trained to communicate. On commercial television, these on-location reporters are usually young, attractive people, who have been primed for their appearance. Hair and make-up done, clothes styled. And the way they speak, as if the end of the world is looming near. Full of drama and suspense. Are they for real? This is life, people, not a soap opera or a Hollywood movie. This is precisely why I cannot watch the news bulletins.

Let's get real for a minute. Anything that goes to air on the news must pass through a certain filter. Is it in the public's interest? Is it controversial? Is it competitive? You can always tell if it has been a slow news day. It's when you see a feel-good story or something without much relevance to the rest of the content. Actually, they don't even do that anymore. They just keep repeating the juicy stuff, over and over again. Don't underestimate, either, the content which appears to be news but is really just commercial in nature. Trust me, I know!

Now back to this particular example. In my opinion, the presenter took an unsolicited swing at the premier, and made her look weak and indecisive. This was done deliberately and out of ego. The question was not relevant to the rest of the interview, and considering everything else going on at that time, was totally misplaced. I am sure the premier, and the rest of the country, had more important issues going on.

And it is an important issue. But was that really the time to discuss it, in the context of current events?

We all know that women are the minority in positions of leadership, and politics is no exception. We know that misogyny exists among the ranks of parliament, as it does in most places of work. We have all seen the likes of former prime minister, Julia Gillard, and former foreign minister, Julie Bishop, battle those same demons, and we all know what happened to their careers. One can understand the difficult position this leader found herself in at that very moment. Imagine she had called it out. That would have become the topic of the next few news cycles and would have overshadowed much of the work she was doing to lead her state through the prevailing crisis. It was not the time to exert this sort of pressure on leaders. I think it was out of line to put her in that position.

I have always liked this particular presenter's style, but I must say that after I saw this interview, it did leave a bitter taste in my mouth. The media should work to present the facts in a way which is unbiased and fair. Why is it that, as humans, we are expected to treat other humans with respect and dignity, but it seems that if you are a politician or in the media, you are exempt from those rules.

This particular attack on the premier was underhanded and unfair. And when she didn't get the answer she was looking for, the presenter continued to pursue it relentlessly. Do you know why she did that? She did it for her own ego. For her own ratings. For her own career.

The public are starting to see through the garbage. I am not a resident of that particular state, and nor am I aligned with any political party. I am indifferent to that premier as a politician, but I am considerate of her as a human being. So, what gives me the right to comment on these issues? Well, the fact that I believe everyone, irrespective of who they are or what they do, deserves a fair go.

And right now, we should be thanking and supporting our leaders because they have the toughest jobs to do and the most difficult decisions to make. It is very easy for us to sit back and judge, but from our narrow view of the world, we don't have all the facts and can't see the big picture. We criticise because that's what we do. We want to see people fall and fail, instead of triumphing and succeeding. We don't support people; we do our best to tear them down. We like the drama; it feeds our egos.

I used to think I would like to be in politics. My strong sense of service and social justice has always made this an area of interest to me. But, given that in reality, it rarely has anything to do with either of these, my inability to strategise effectively, to play games, and to want to see people fail, would certainly set me up for instant disappointment.

Whether you like them or despise them or disagree with their handling of the situation right now, I wouldn't want to be carrying the burden and responsibility of our leaders. We do not have the right to judge others until we have walked a mile in their shoes. In the interview with the NSW premier, this presenter lost her credibility in my eyes. Her relentless pursuit of the next big headline put a person who is obviously under much strain, in an awkward position. The premier was damned if she did and damned if she didn't.

There has been much commentary on this interview, with much division. Sure, the premier's answers made her look like a politician. That is what she is. What would we have expected her to say under the circumstances? The presenter, on the other hand, allowed her ego to get the better of her, transforming her usual attractive face into that of a wild dingo in search of its next prey.

But she was dead right; we do need to call out inappropriate behaviour when it happens. And there is a hell of a lot of bad behaviour going around right now!

So, let's get real. Let's learn to challenge what we are being told if it just doesn't sit right. Your gut knows the truth, as I have said in an earlier chapter; your ego is the one that buys into the fear. That part is being manufactured. My hope is that we can all become more discerning and begin to see the power we all have within us, rather than believing the people who try to tell us that we are powerless and therefore we have no choice but to follow them.

I personally don't like things that are manufactured. I also don't like fake or cheap knock-offs, whether in people or in handbags. If I can't afford or attract the real deal, I prefer to go without. That's just me. Always true to who I am, and never tempted to be anything else.

And speaking of fake pretending to be real, there is no greater example of this than our social media platforms. Please be mindful of this and proceed with caution. Use it as a tool to spread positivity rather than to fuel fear and judge others from a distance. Let's teach our kids to use it properly and make more appropriate choices. Let's use it for its intended purpose, to connect us with the people we love and don't often get a chance to see. And there is no better time to start doing this than right now.

FOLLOW THE LEADER

In my book *Who Switched the Lights On?* I dedicated a chapter to the topic of leadership. In it, I discussed what real leadership looks like to me, and what the opposite looks like, and how it affects us. Leadership is being put under the spotlight right now. The true test of leadership is how events like these current ones are being handled. Last time I talked about daring leadership; this time I want to talk about authentic leadership.

I am passionate about this topic, because all around me, I am continuing to see examples of where there is a clear abuse of power and where we allow egomaniacs to run the show. I also see examples of inspirational leadership that gives me a glimmer of hope for the future.

I am not sure if you have noticed lately, but there appears to be a steady dismantling of the structures that have governed us for so long. The past few months have seen the failure of some of the most powerful institutions, institutions which on the surface appeared bulletproof. We have also seen the widespread stepping down of some of the world's most highly paid heads of organisations.

Why is this happening?

This current covid-19 crisis is shining a light on the things that are no longer working or serving us. These things are becoming clearer, and they need to change or be removed completely. Let's take the situation in Victoria's private-sector aged care as an example. Where is the leadership in this sector and who thinks it is acceptable to put the lives of people in jeopardy in order to make a profit? It is heartbreaking to watch all of this unfold around us. To see footage of families being told that their loved ones are well and resting when in fact they were dying in hospital is devastating. To allow someone to die alone, without dignity, would have to be one of the cruellest things we can do to someone. Since when is aged care something to make a buck from? Where is the *care* in aged care? This is precisely what happens when we privatise something that should not be made private. We open it up to competition and potential short cuts, rather than providing what is actually required for people at this stage of their lives. In my opinion, aged care belongs in the not-for-profit sector. Simple!

The aged care example is just one of many. But it is a good example of how things can go terribly wrong when you take your eye off the ball and allow too many people to play in the team, people who are really not interested in being a team player. Greedy people seek out opportunity and let's face it, an ageing population provides ample opportunity. They also prey on weaknesses, and let's face it, this is a vulnerable sector. Why else do you think there are so many aged care facilities sprouting up all over the place? And while it is terribly sad that people have died because of these circumstances, I for one am pleased that these sectors are finally being exposed and their failings brought to light. At least now that we are aware of the problem, we can work towards a solution which looks after the ones that really matter, the people. Hopefully, we can now provide the care that they so rightly deserve and in doing so, save many more lives in the process. For it is only once things come to light that you can do something about them.

In my opinion, it is definitely time for change. No longer can we continue to run organisations and governments without any regard for our most important resource: people. And it is the leaders who are authentic in their actions, who are selfless and who genuinely value their people, who are capable of sustaining their leadership into the next phase.

The prerequisite for being an effective leader is to have people who buy into a vision and therefore choose to follow a leader. It is much less about the individual who is leading, and much more about the vision and the way it is presented to constituents.

Give someone who is not a true leader a title, and add to that a financial bonus or incentive, and watch the ego take off on its own tangent, with absolutely no regard for who it takes out along the way. The victims are seen merely as the collateral damage of fulfilling self-serving goals. This might sound drastic to those who have not worked in the corporate world. Those of you who have, know that my description is indeed accurate.

The hallmark of a true leader is seen in times of crisis. These times provide the perfect opportunity for true leaders to step up and show us what they are made of. While it is a terrible thing to have to deal with a crisis, it is in these adverse times that a leader is presented with an opportunity to leave their mark on history. I must say that despite what you may think of our elected leaders on any given day, they have had a challenging job of leading during this covid-19 crisis.

Internationally, Jacinda Ardern, the prime minister of New Zealand, continues to govern in her unique, authentic and grounded way. There is no denying that I am a big fan of hers, and that's not only because she is a woman. I have heard men refer to her as weak merely because she is a woman. And to those men, their attitude adequately shows how threatened they are by strong, intelligent women, who are so natural in the way they lead that it appears they were indeed born for the job. Jacinda

Ardern is able to lead in an empathetic way because she is intelligent, both intellectually and emotionally. She is brave, and she is in the job for the right reasons: to represent the people and not herself. And much of that superpower is precisely because she is a woman!

Has anybody noticed that during this crisis there has not been much coverage of the opposition? It appears that both sides of our government, apart from the odd rebuttal or two, are actually working together to get us through these challenges. These are unprecedented times (and isn't that another of the most used word of 2020?) and perhaps our leaders are finally figuring out that it is in the country's best interest to work together towards solutions which are best for the collective. It is a refreshing change and brings me back to a question I pose in my first book, *Who Switched the Lights On?* What is the need for the 'opposition'?

Wouldn't bipartisanship be a much better approach? But no, that wouldn't work. You know why? Because in this world, there have to be winners and losers. Which is simply not the truth. I believe there is enough to go around so each of us wins to some extent. That is the difference between having an outlook of abundance rather than one of lack. When the view is one of lack, there is a belief that one has to fight for one's rightful share of resources, rather than seeing that there is indeed enough to go around.

But the silence of the opposition doesn't ever last long, because there is not much drama in everyone getting along and working towards a common goal. And as I write this, the tables are starting to turn on our leaders. Some things have gone wrong and some decisions have come back to haunt them, which was inevitable in such a large-scale event. And suddenly the opposition are coming out of the woodwork, not to help them fix it because our livelihood is at stake, but to keep driving home the message of the government's incompetence. We all know what went wrong. We can't change it. We need solutions, not point scoring. Our lives are not a game. This is serious business and we are suffering badly. I couldn't give a damn about talking about a problem I can't solve. I want to hear what they propose to do about it!

It has been interesting to watch how different leaders respond in the face of a crisis. And there is nothing more confronting than the comments of Donald Trump, current president of the United States. Imagine you were employed to be on his advisory team? Could you imagine? You would spend every day fighting fires and holding your breath every time he opened his mouth or picked up his phone to tweet. There's not much advising going on, I would say. This man has a mind of his own and he doesn't care too much for the consequences of his actions. I hope those poor people on his staff are being well compensated for the unenviable task of working with this president.

I am currently reading a book by John Bolton, former national security adviser to President Trump. This book suggests that it's much worse than you can even imagine, which is why he eventually had to resign from his role. It's fascinating how a person like Trump could even qualify to become the president of one of the world's most powerful countries, with no prior experience in politics. Either I am not seeing the full picture here, or money and ego have much more influence than even I can imagine. Or perhaps it really does take a businessman to run the country, someone who cares little about political alliances. With the US elections nearing, at the time of writing this book, I watch intently as the situation continues to unfold.

The average person has to jump through hoops to qualify for a decent job. Me included. But it sounds like it would be easier to apply for the presidency of the US if recent examples like Donald Trump are anything to go by. The world has certainly gone completely mad. The office which should be held to the highest standard of integrity and should be a role model to the rest of the world is being made to look like an absolute circus. Isn't it amazing how money can even make clowns look like less frightening than they really are!

Clowns, chameleons, it's getting harder to see what's real. Mutton dressed as lamb. The fakes are doing a really good job at disguising themselves and trying to blend in with the real people.

FROM INSIDE MY COCOON

It's comfortable and warm in my little cocoon. And I won't be emerging for a little while longer. Not until I am ready. Much has to happen before I can venture outside. I tried to come out a little while ago; I thought it was time. I was ready to make the necessary adjustments. I knew the world would look a little different from how it did before I went into hibernation. But it proved to be unsafe. The world was not yet prepared, and my wings were not quite strong enough to enable me to fly. There was still some work to be done. Patience is a virtue. One cannot rush the process. It's better to trust the timing of things. When it's time, I will know. I will feel it in my gut. I will have transformed into the person I need to be in order to take my rightful place in the world. And I will be ready.

From inside the cocoon where I currently sit, I have a unique view of what is going on outside, and of the many different aspects of our current circumstances. In times gone by, I would have been immersed in the world of corporate business and consumed by the effects on that particular sector.

But from where I sit now, it's warm and safe, and my view of the world is wider. So far, my family and I are healthy, and although I know indirectly of a few people who have contracted the virus, nobody close to me has had their health affected by it. But still the numbers continue to grow, with no relief in sight. It's August now and we are at full lockdown, and one wonders where it could possibly go from here. Surely, we have hit rock bottom already.

Mentally, it is quite a different story. We are all surrounded by people who have been affected in so many ways, ways which have nothing at all to do with their physical health. Emotionally, mentally and financially, we are all being challenged, some to the point of despair.

What am I seeing from my vantage point? I am seeing how absolutely everything is connected. How when you tinker with one thing, it affects the next thing. And that, in turn, affects something else, creating a vicious cycle and causing a ripple effect throughout the entire world. This pandemic has shown us that no man is an island. That every one of our actions has an effect on the next person, and the one after that. Each of us represents a link in a very long chain. We are all connected, and so is everything else.

What it also does, is that it exposes things that are no longer serving humanity, the structures that break down under new pressures. And while it is true that we are dealing with a virus, we are actually seeing how contagious many other things are, and how, if they are not stopped, they can spiral out of control.

This virus keeps opening up a new set of issues. Much like a set of Russian matryoshka (nesting) dolls, just when you think you have reached the end, you discover another little surprise. Each doll brings about its own set of consequences, exposing things we couldn't see before. And because everything is so intricately connected, it takes a lot of skill to sort through the pieces and put things back together again.

We need to learn from these events and change the way we do things. We need to be looking after our individual selves much more, being more creative and reinventing ourselves in the face of change. We need to be looking after our society and in particular those who are most vulnerable. We need to re-establish our sense of community and replace what we have now, which is 'each man for himself'. We need to take a longer-term view and make more appropriate investments in our future. We need to consider what we need in order to go forward.

The fact that we have been unable to combat a virus has left us exposed. This potentially opens us up to the need to invest more in science in order to be more prepared the next time around. Because there will be a next time. History tells us that. We should also be more mindful of which of our foreign neighbours we rely on, and we should be investing in our own capabilities and work towards becoming more self-sufficient. We should consider carefully who and what we allow to penetrate our borders.

When we consider shareholders, we need to redefine this category. Who are the real shareholders in the world? Not only are they the ones who contribute financially to an organisation, but they are the ones who invest other things into it. This category should be expanded to include customers, employees, community and the environment itself, as it too supplies some of the resources. Only when we come to realise that these are the groups we are in fact working for, will we understand that we have a duty to deliver to each of the shareholder groups. That will have a significant impact on the way we conduct business in future.

We need to become more ethical. More equitable. We need to take into account the human cost of our decisions. Like everything else at the moment, we are being asked to reflect on where we are at and decide where we want to go and how we want to get there. Gone are the days of just accepting how certain things are done. Now is the time to ask questions. Why does it have to be this way? Why can't it be done differently?

In my experience, when I have taken the time to ask the appropriate questions, people have opened up to me and told me the truth. What I found is that most people who work in middle management or below in an organisation do not feel as though they have a voice; rarely do they feel listened to or considered. They feel powerless to affect decision-making, even though they are the ones who are at the grassroots of an organisation. Many think that knowledge is power, and they therefore try to hold onto it for dear life. Knowledge is only powerful if it is shared and acted on in a way that serves the collective. Rather than just accepting the way things have always been done, we have to step up and be part of the solution.

In no way am I professing to be an expert in these matters. My ideas stem from what I believe. They are based on my past experiences, and also on my current, objective view of what is going on. But it may all be easy for me to say from the comfort of my little cocoon. All I can hope is that some of these ideas sow a seed of hope for our collective future.

A GLIMMER OF LIGHT

One of the first things I do each morning, besides turning on the coffee machine, is to open all of the blinds in my house. Every single one. Not a little bit, or part of the way, but right to the top. I do this to let the light pour in.

I have always been this way. I like clarity and transparency. I want to be able to see what I am dealing with. In direct contrast, I grew up in a house that structurally didn't allow much light in, apart from some windows which opened onto an indoor garden, but rarely allowed the warmth in. The rest of the windows in the house—and it was a substantial home—had coverings on them, which for the most part remained closed. For some reason my family liked it this way. I was the opposite.

We need both the dark and the light. The light is more obvious and much more pronounced when it is dark. The contrast is deeper. Its power is much greater, and often it has to work harder to drive out the dark. But light will always prevail. It is stronger and more luminescent, and can create much more energy than its extreme counterpart.

The world we are currently living in needs the light more than it has ever needed it before. For it is only this that has the power to lift the dark veil which threatens to overshadow our every day, taking our livelihood, our freedoms, our physical and mental health, our passion and our zest for life. But that's all the dark can do. It can threaten, create fear and incite drama, but the choice to give it our power lies with us. We choose whether we give in to the dark or whether we keep the faith, knowing that the reset switch is what we need to find, in order to illuminate the way forward.

There are many examples of light and dark, particularly at the moment.

During this downtime, I have been a little concerned about my own level of productivity. I am used to working at a fast pace, so much so that I don't really know what to do when things slow down. And when they have come to a crashing halt, then what?

I can be quite hard on myself. After all, I am well-versed in the concept of expectation. But it seems I impose them on myself, all by myself, according to what I think those expectations are likely to be. When things are slow, I tend to go into the procrastination phase. And I have been known to stay there for quite some time. When I get moving, however, I have the ability to pick up speed at an impressive rate.

I have been at home since mid-March (it is now almost the middle of August). I have been officially without work since April. I have never been without work in my entire adult life, until now. I had a choice. Lose myself or get comfortable in my new zone. So, I did the latter, even though on some days, I did in fact lose myself for a little while. From day to day it seems that not much gets done. You just know that you could have done more. This is the old pattern of conditioning that I have been accustomed to. I can now see the fault in those particular patterns. To me, stress, speed and time spent on a task equated to productivity—that of a quality standard. I have now seen that the opposite can also be true and can produce an equal or even higher standard of quality. Remaining calm and taking the time, without the stress, can not only achieve a positive outcome, but can be a much more enjoyable process.

When I look back over the time that has passed, even though at times it feels like it is standing still, I can see just how productive I have been. In fact, I have been more productive than usual, and have managed to attract many more positive things. The negative things that have happened to me over the past few months are starting to fade, like a distant memory. I have been extremely creative. I have spent quality time with my children and a few friends. I have made a conscious effort to exercise more and invest more time in myself. I have learnt a great deal. I have read more books than I have read in a long time. I have decided to further my education, going through the application and interview process, and being accepted into an MBA program. This is huge for me. I have published my first book and produced all of the items required for its launch and promotion. I have also written this entire book during this time and made good progress on two others.

I have rested. Replenished. Exercised. Indulged. Reflected. Rejuvenated.

I know the story is not the same for all of us. In some circumstances in our society, it is becoming increasingly difficult to see the light. And I feel for people who are trapped in these situations. My fear is that the casualties indirectly resulting from this crisis will not be documented as they should be, as a direct result and consequence. Nor will they make the evening news, although they are very much part of the official statistics, and even more devastating.

While this time has not been easy for most, upon reflection, for my part, I am extremely grateful for the time I have had to do the things I have always dreamt of doing and had never found the time to do. I am thankful for the time I have had to carry out my personal reset.

Where to from here?

Each day reveals a new contradiction and a new uncertainty. Every day that passes makes the isolation heavier than the day before. On those days, a shift of energy is what is required. We need to shift our focus through exercise or by engaging in an interest that provides joy or uplift. Often this can be found in the simplest of activities. It is important to maintain connections during this time. And it is a good time to remove yourself from toxic people if you can. Nothing will ever be quite the same again, and this period of time is the segue into whatever comes next. This is the pause before the reset. What is on the other side, while it is very much unknown, will be very much what we choose to make it.

I have become unplugged from many of the things in my life I thought I needed. Perhaps I was attached to them because I didn't fully realise my own self-worth and my ability to be autonomous. I allowed myself to become defined by others, and when I lost those things, I was confronted with a slight identity crisis. One of the greatest lessons I have learnt is not to become attached to places or things, only to a vision and a purpose.

The last ten years of my journey have been stitched together by periods of significant awakening and the necessary lessons which followed as a result of the lights being switched on. Much of my learning has taken place during that time. Entering this new phase, although things were looking brighter, inevitably, I was left with a few remaining cobwebs that needed to be swept away. Many of these were attachments to things that no longer served me, the removal of which only occurred once I rediscovered my own sense of worth, and the faith and courage to continue on a forward journey without being tempted to doubt my decisions or look back over my shoulder to the past. And just to make sure I was committed to the process, these latest challenges, which were mostly the direct result of the worldwide phenomenon known as covid-19, were sent my way just to seal the deal. And inevitably, each of those challenges has caused me to have a good talking to my shadow self, leading to enlightening discussions and sometimes quite heavy debates.

I feel like I have been in and out of the rabbit hole so many times over the past year that I have developed a sensitivity to extreme emotions. It feels much like being on a rollercoaster. You are forever holding your breath because you're not quite sure what lies ahead or how the next bend in the track will affect you. You are continuously braced for impact. What I have learnt, however, is that the ride is much more enjoyable if you loosen your grip and relax into it, embracing the uncertainty of what lies ahead, and turning it into excitement.

For all of the things that I have become unplugged from—people, work, relationships—there are other things I have become more plugged into. And perhaps that is precisely what this period has been all about. Perhaps it is the time that each of us, along with the entire planet, and the planet itself, needed in order to attempt to repair the fault, the malfunction, the power surge, by unplugging every single item in our lives from its socket, and turning off every single light. Allowing everything to recover for a little while before we can eventually reach for the switch that is going to reset everything to better than new, and brighter and more radiant than it has ever been before.

My hope is that you manage to hit that reset switch in a way that makes you value and appreciate all of the things that it will have the power to illuminate, including your faith and your belief in the power you have to change the world.

Despite everything that has happened in the past year, your energy is still as radiant as it has ever been. Your crown is still as shiny and well deserved. Give it a little polish and put it back on. Go forth and use it to power up a better-looking world.

I am not afraid of the dark. And there is no need for you to be afraid of it either.

> *I have loved the stars too fondly to be fearful of the night.*
>
> SARAH WILLIAMS, *Twilight Hours: A Legacy of Verse*

EPILOGUE

For most of us, it all began on 31 December 2019. As the world prepared to farewell 2019, China reported a new coronavirus emerging from the Wuhan province. The world is still unaware of just how long it took for China to disclose this fact. There have been conflicting reports as to who China's patient zero was. Some reports identified the patient as a shrimp merchant at the Huanan Seafood Market in Wuhan. Two thirds of early cases were traced back to the popular live animal wet market. It has been alleged that the virus may have been transmitted to humans through live bats.[10]

Other reports from China suggest the virus did not start at the wet markets but had been spreading slowly among residents before it was linked to the market outbreak. We may never know what really happened, and fortunately, the solution is not contingent on finding patient zero.[11]

It has also been widely reported that the doctor who first warned of the virus died in hospital in February 2020.[12] In December 2019, Dr Li Wenliang, aged thirty-four, warned his medical school classmates of a mystery illness that had him and many others quarantined in hospital. A few days after sending out this message, he allegedly received a visit by authorities who asked him to sign a document stating that he had engaged in illegal behaviour by spreading the message.[13]

Upon alerting the world of the virus, the Chinese Government moved to lockdown Wuhan, a city of 11 million people, in attempt to try to prevent the spread of the disease. Because it was a newly mutated virus, humans had no immunity to it, and there was no vaccine or specific treatment. It was highly contagious and everyone was susceptible.

But it was already proving too late for the rest of the world. The lunar new year helped to spread the coronavirus globally as hundreds of millions of Chinese people travelled home or abroad during the holiday period. All of this at a time when, on the global stage, The United States was threatening sanctions on China and Trump himself prepares to contest an election in November 2020. All of this may be unrelated of course, but one must admit that these are interesting times.

On 11 February 2020, the World Health Organization (WHO), officially named the disease 'COVID-19'. Coronaviruses are a family of viruses, most of which are harmless to humans. Four types are known to cause common colds, and two others can cause severe lung infections. Covid-19 appears to be more similar to what we have seen in the past with SARS. SARS—severe acute respiratory syndrome—is a viral respiratory illness caused by a coronavirus. It is a contagious and potentially fatal disease. An outbreak of SARS occurred in 2002–2003 but it is no longer circulating. This disease was also reported to have originated in Asia.

One month after naming the virus, WHO declared the covid-19 outbreak a pandemic. A pandemic is an epidemic that has travelled internationally, infecting a great number of people. The controls for managing a pandemic are much more challenging than those for an epidemic. Most at risk are those whose health may be compromised by other factors, in particular the elderly. Interestingly, the spread among children has been minor.

At the time of writing this epilogue (September 2020), the city where I live (Melbourne, Australia) is currently dealing with the second wave of the virus. Although by world standards the numbers are still relatively low, the restrictions being used to combat the spread are unprecedented and draconian, and have been described as being among the most stringent in the world. We are in complete lockdown. We are only allowed to leave our homes for one hour a day to exercise, or to go to the supermarket. Masks are compulsory when outdoors and we are all required to respect a curfew, which comes into effect each evening at 8 p.m. As of today (14 September) the curfew has been extended by one hour to reflect the increase in daylight hours.

By 13 September 2020 the world had seen over 29 million cases of covid-19, of which there were 927 thousand deaths (or 4 per cent); 21 million people had recovered.

As of this day, there are just over seven million active cases around the world; 99 per cent of these are said to be mild cases, with 1 per cent considered serious or critical.[14] The side effects or any long-term adverse health effects are not known at this stage but there have been reports of ongoing complications in some cases. The highest number of cases have been experienced in the US, with over 6.7 million infected and 198 thousand deaths.[15]

When I was researching these numbers, I found it interesting to compare the death rates in many Western and first world countries to those being experienced in developing or third world nations, taking into account that the rates of testing differ in each country, with more sophisticated techniques in developed countries identifying a greater number of cases. But still, we should be seeing a greater rate of recovery in more developed countries that have access to better healthcare and sanitation. But the opposite seems to be true.

The US, with the highest number of infections in the world, had a death rate of 3 per cent. That is, of the people infected, 3 per cent did not recover. In China, where the outbreak first originated, there were 85 thousand cases and a death rate of 5.4 per cent. Then there are countries such as Italy, France, the United Kingdom, Belgium, Hungary and the Netherlands whose death rates were all up around 10 per cent. One could argue that they may have an ageing population, but these numbers still seem extremely high to me.

Among the countries to handle the crisis well was Singapore, which experienced 57 thousand cases and had 27 deaths. Although all deaths are serious, this number is negligible. Singapore is one of the countries which has the highest rate of testing at 39 per cent of the population. In comparison, Australia's testing rate is 27 per cent, which is at the same level of testing as the US. Another notable example is Taiwan, a country with a similar population to Australia. There the cases were 498 with seven deaths. The rate of testing has been very low at 3.7 per cent of the population. If we look at both Singapore and Taiwan, each of these countries appear to have acted early and swiftly with good handling of contract tracing and handling of cases.[16]

Closer to my home, Australia and New Zealand, both had matters relatively under control. New Zealand had 1797 cases with 24 deaths, a rate of 1.3 per cent, and in Australia, the number of infected is just over 26 thousand with a death rate of 3 per cent, most of which have been contributed by my home state of Victoria. Prior to the second wave in Victoria, Australia had a death rate of 1 per cent. Here in Victoria we now seem to be coming out of a very dark period in which we have experienced extremely high new daily case numbers, while the rest of the country has a low number of new cases per day. The major contributing factors to the situation in Victoria are believed to have been the mishandling of hotel quarantining for passengers arriving from overseas and a crisis in the aged care sector.

As an indication of the difference between the situation in Victoria compared to the rest of Australia, as of 14 September, of the 26 thousand cases, 19,835 have been in Victoria. Of the total national deaths of 810, most (723) were from Victoria. For the purposes of comparison, the state with the next highest number of cases is New South Wales with 4166 cases and 52 deaths,[17] with some of these resulting from the *Ruby Princess* disembarkation.[18]

This crisis is far from over. Borders continue to remain shut, completely crippling the tourism industry. There is much to be done before we can take the necessary steps to recovery. For now, they are baby steps, and we hope to have come through the worst of it. The fact is, however, that we may never completely eradicate this virus. We may or may not find a vaccine. This is another complex issue in itself. And if we do, will we all be forced to be vaccinated? I hope it will not come to that.

It is my hope that our governments will work to open us up for business sooner rather than later and find ways of managing what will remain of this pandemic, even if just for the short term. In the long term, I hope they look at this time as an opportunity to improve the way we do things and work more collectively to reach our desired outcomes, outcomes that promote prosperity, health and wellbeing for everyone, in place of greed, materialism and self-serving interests.

Together, let's work towards a better future and take care of our people and our planet. Because those two things need one another in order to survive. It's a partnership.

ENDNOTES

1 AO Bell & A McNeillie (eds), *The diary of Virginia Woolf*, vol. 3, *1925–1930*, Harcourt Brace Jovanovich, New York, 1980, p. 107.

2 L Richard, N Brew & L Smith, *2019–20 Australian bushfires—frequently asked questions: a quick guide*, Parliament of Australia, Canberra, 12 March 2020. https://www.aph.gov.au/About_Parliament/Parliamentary_Departments/Parliamentary_Library/pubs/rp/rp1920/Quick_Guides/AustralianBushfires

3 B Plumer, 'Nine facts about terrorism in the United States since 9/11', *Washington Post*, 12 September 2013. https://www.washingtonpost.com/news/wonk/wp/2013/09/11/nine-facts-about-terrorism-in-the-united-states-since-911/

4 History.com editors, *Spanish flu*, 12 October 2010, updated 19 May 2020. https://www.history.com/topics/world-war-i/1918-flu-pandemic

5 Australian Government Department of Health, *Australian influenza surveillance report and activity updates*, Canberra, 11 September 2020. https://www1.health.gov.au/internet/main/publishing.nsf/Content/cda-surveil-ozflu-flucurr.htm

6 T Cassidy, 'Flu season which struck down 310,000 Australians "worst on record" due to early outbreaks', *ABC Sunshine Coast*, 11 February 2020. https://www.abc.net.au/news/2020-02-11/early-outbreaks-to-blame-for-worst-flu-season-on-record/11949320

7 Black Dog Institute, *Facts about suicide in Australia*, Sydney, n.d. (accessed 21 September 2020). https://www.blackdoginstitute.org.au/resources-support/suicide-self-harm/facts-about-suicide-in-australia/

8 Life in Mind Australia, *Suicide facts and stats*, Newcastle, NSW, n.d. (accessed 21 September 2020). https://lifeinmind.org.au/about-suicide/suicide-data/suicide-facts-and-stats

9 Conservation International, 'Nature is speaking—Julia Roberts is Mother Nature',

YouTube, 5 October 2014. https://youtu.be/WmVLcj-XKnM

10 P Williams, L Stein & R Armitage, 'The coronavirus "patient zero" set off a chain of events which upturned the lives of 7 billion people', *ABC News*, 23 April 2020. https://www.abc.net.au/news/2020-04-23/how-coronavirus-went-from-patient-zero-to-the-world/12165336

11 J Seidel, 'Scientists rush to find "Patient Zero" in a bid to stop the coronavirus', *News.com.au*, 1 February 2020. https://www.news.com.au/lifestyle/health/health-problems/scientists-rush-to-find-patient-zero-in-a-bid-to-stop-the-coronavirus/news-story/47ed87486e5b40ec5123dc66acea675f

12 2020: the year the world changed forever. The abbreviations BC and AD could take on a whole new meaning: Before Covid and Anno Dopo (Italian for 'the year after').

13 'Li Wenliang: coronavirus death of Wuhan doctor sparks anger', *BBC News*, 7 February 2020. https://www.bbc.com/news/world-asia-china-51409801

14 'Covid-19 coronavirus pandemic', *Worldometer* (accessed 13 September 2020). https://www.worldometers.info/coronavirus/

15 'Coronavirus statistics: Australia', *epidemic-stats.com* (accessed 13 September 2020). https://epidemic-stats.com/coronavirus/australia

16 A Rogers, 'Singapore was ready for covid-19—other countries, take note', *Wired*, 12 March 2020. https://www.wired.com/story/singapore-was-ready-for-covid-19-other-countries-take-note/

17 Australian Government Department of Health, *Coronavirus (COVID-19) current situation and case numbers*, Canberra (accessed 13 September 2020). https://www.health.gov.au/news/health-alerts/novel-coronavirus-2019-ncov-health-alert/coronavirus-covid-19-current-situation-and-case-numbers

18 S Thomas, 'NSW coronavirus death toll rises, with three people dying after travelling on the Ruby Princess', *ABC News*, 5 April 2020. https://www.abc.net.au/news/2020-04-05/nsw-health-reports-four-more-coronavirus-deaths/12122966

ABOUT THE AUTHOR

Pina Di Donato is an avid philanthropist, business person, highly experienced marketing professional and author. She is the author of *Who Switched the Lights On?* and the co-author of the history and business book, *A Long Way from Home*.

She has held many board positions with not-for-profit organisations, including being deputy chair of Northern Health Foundation and having established a pivotal charity arm while helping to rebuild one of the largest poultry producers in Australia.

Passionate about sharing her experiences through storytelling, Pina hopes to inspire others to step out of their comfort zone and onto the path of fulfilling their own unique purpose.

Pina lives in Melbourne, Australia, with her three children.

www.ingramcontent.com/pod-product-compliance
Lightning Source LLC
Chambersburg PA
CBHW020320010526
44107CB00054B/1914